BONSAI
For Beginners

A Fundamental and Complete Guide:
Techniques of
Cultivation, Wiring, Pruning
Diseases and Care of Bonsai Tree

Akira Kobayashi

小林明

BONSAI
Table of Contents

Introduction

Bonsai is a special art form used in Japan where live trees are grown in pots or containers. Similar practices exist in other Eastern cultures, but because of the peaceful tranquility of these practices, many of them have been adopted across the world. The term "bonsai" is a rather broad term, but directly translated it means miniature potted trees.

Bonsai are not difficult to care for, it is enough to love plants, understand their needs and respect that balance that is typical of Bonsai.

Remember that we can make life in a vase that normally lives in huge spaces. Bonsai is balanced and when this aspect fails, when the set of forces that create it is broken, our plant could die, and this is the last thing we want. In fact, you will read in the following pages that the plant, under certain conditions, can't survive; not to scare you but, unfortunately, this could happen as an extreme case, but you will also understand over time, that it is not so easy to make a tree die. Do not worry about all the techniques explained here, just think that you are a beginner now and that, when time and quantity are mastered, everything will become extremely easy. In this manual we will see together, step by step, the systems, techniques, ways, and tricks to ensure that your tree keeps you company over several years, encouraging you to practice and study more and more.

There are many reasons why someone would want to grow or own a bonsai. Even though it's a practice that takes a lot of patience, gentleness, and understanding, it is one of the most rewarding practices or hobbies that anyone could try. Nurturing a bonsai isn't something to be taken lightly because it does take time and effort, but those who do embark on this tranquil journey of growth and discovering peace are never disappointed.

This book is divided into different sections and even though it will take time to work through each one, all of these techniques are designed for beginners. Bonsais have increased in popularity and can be found relatively easily in large gardening stores, in specialty shops, and online. Some enthusiasts like to have trees that are already established, but you might find that you would like to grow your bonsai from a seed or seedling. The latter can be more rewarding, but it does take years of patience.

Whichever you choose, you won't be disappointed in learning how to grow, cultivate, and nurture your very own bonsai.

The term bonsai, from the Japanese bon (pot) and sai (tree), indicates an art form that allows you to grow miniature trees and plants, through meticulous daily care.

Originally, the bonsai spread to China where the skill of the masters reached the point of creating real tiny landscapes populated by mountains, rivers, houses, and people.

It is said that the poet Guen-Ming, in the fourth century after Christ, had retired to devote himself to planting and caring for chrysanthemums in some containers, thus starting the cultivation of plants in pots.

Two hundred years later, a new art was created in China, the Pen-Jin, as shown by various paintings of the Tang Dynasty (618-906), depicting dwarf trees used as ornaments.

During the 14th century, under the Ming Dynasty, bonsai were already widespread and were cultivated giving life to various styles.

However, bonsai is not only born as an aesthetic requirement but also as a spiritual exercise, as a search for harmony between man and nature, within the principles of the Zen discipline. The bonsai artist tests himself, brings his inner world closer to the outer one, trying to imprison and regulate the millennial forces of nature. In following his art, he is guided by the Zen concepts of naturalness, simplicity, harmony, and concentration on the essential.

When bonsai arrived in Japan, as a gift from wealthy Chinese, it fascinated the aristocracy precisely because of its spiritual intensity, thus becoming one of the nobility's favorite art forms. For Japan, this was the period of the spread of Zen Buddhism, during the Heian era, between the eighth and twelfth centuries.

But there is another version of the history of the Japanese art of growing bonsai.

The art of cultivating bonsais may be an ancient practice, but Japan isn't where it originally began. Bonsai cultivation was adopted from the Chinese practice of penjing, which also involves growing miniature trees in pots and small containers.

From as early as the sixth century, personnel from the Chinese Imperial Embassy and Japanese students of Buddhism traveled to mainland China where they returned with tree seedlings in potted containers as souvenirs. The Japanese students went on 17 missions to China between the years of 603 and 839 where they not only kept returning with these souvenirs, they also gained a lot of knowledge on how to cultivate them from the Tang court.

The philosophy and primary purpose of growing these trees is to bring a sense of peace and awe for the grower and anyone who gazes upon it. Once the monks started to realize how beautiful these little creations were and how pleasant it was to grow these potted trees, they instantly fell in love with the whole process. Growing bonsais was an unusual custom because plants were usually grown during those time periods to either provide food or medicine, but bonsais provided neither of these.   But the real reason for growing bonsai has a much different meaning than merely growing plants for food or medicine and has a much deeper spiritual and emotional meaning behind it.

CHAPTER 1

The Principles Of Bonsai Art

Bonsai are perfectly normal plants, which in nature would grow normally and which would be several meters high, depending on the species; pure gardening techniques are what allow us to keep an old oak on our windowsill, inside a vase. While we're at it, let's dispel another myth, according to which Bonsai suffer.

Any operation that is done to a tree to make it small is bloodless for the plant itself, for many reasons, including the fact that plants have no nervous system and, therefore, do not have the ability to feel pain.

Moreover, it is well known that, for example, fruit trees, to produce more fruit, require numerous pruning, which does not make the tree suffer but on the contrary, stimulates it to produce more.

In short, the only reaction that a tree or any other plant has consequently to the cutting of a part of it is the production of other branches or other leaves to replace what is lost.

And then it is logical that all these techniques are not used to make the plant die but to make it live long and healthy.

The bonsai artist cultivates and takes care of his creation in a small container and trying to reproduce a glimpse of nature inside his home, which preserves the harmony of proportions, despite being significantly reduced in size.

He tries to draw its entire splendor from the plant, placing it in a landscape that resembles the real one for everything and enhancing its shape and qualities.

Like any plastic art, bonsai must also respect the basic principles of form, line, texture, space and color. The bonsai artist must always keep these concepts in mind to give value to his creation.

The form is any characteristic or structure that identifies a particular object. Even trees have their own shape, typical of the species they belong to; populate forests, woods and grasslands, adapting to the most diverse climates. Shapes and scenarios that we must strive to recreate in our bonsai.

The line establishes the border or boundary within which a work of art is created. For bonsai, limits are defined by the lines of the container, and the bonsai artist must learn to choose the suitable spatial boundaries within which to place his plant, highlighting its fundamental characteristics.

The texture is the set of structural qualities of a work of art and is born from how an artist works the chosen materials; even bonsai have their own texture, due to the structure of the leaves, the foliage, the trunk, etc.

In some compositions, therefore, some bonsai may be more appropriate than others for the characteristics of their texture: In case you want to highlight the knottiness of a trunk, for example, it is good to choose a tree with a particular bark, or if you want a contrast in the texture, you can combine deciduous trees with evergreen trees.

Space is defined, in art, as the extension that opens in all directions and in the three dimensions, within which things exist.

In bonsai, space is very important, both in the case of compositions, to establish the distance between the trees, and in the case of single trees, in order to obtain the right ratio inside container, space must, therefore, be dosed appropriately, avoiding disproportions or imbalances in the composition.

Finally, color is the sensation due to the stimulation of the retina by the light waves reflected by objects, which thus take on our eyes, particular characteristics and values.

Even bonsai have their colors, not only those of the trunk, leaves and flowers but also those dominant in the various seasons, such as the intermediate shades of the autumn and spring periods. All these elements must be taken into account during the realization of your project.

The bonsai artist must, however, also follow other rules,

which allow you to set the creation and processing of any work of art. Let's talk about balance, rhythm, emphasis and unity.

The balance can be symmetrical or asymmetrical and implies certain stability of the figure. In bonsai art, however, symmetry is considered boring and therefore to be avoided. Rather, we try to give movement to the compositions and we tend to the variety of the form.

Rhythm implies a harmonious succession of the form so that the eye moves through the whole work, without interruption from start to finish.

The rhythm is very important for the bonsai that must hit the eye for its general appearance more than for some details, particularly interesting. The emphasis gives particular relevance to a small part or to an entire area of an object. It can be obtained, either through the decision of the line, or through the specific use of color, or with lighting effects, or through the skillful use of details.

In bonsai, the emphasis can be used to highlight a feature of the plant that we particularly like, which will contribute to the movement of the composition.

Finally, the unit uses color, line, shape, texture and space to obtain a figure that satisfies us as a whole.

To achieve this, it is necessary that each of the elements mentioned completely harmonizes with the others.

By following these principles, a good bonsai artist can manage to obtain a bonsai of excellent value and remarkable value.

The whole process of growing bonsais will start off very similarly to growing any other plant or tree. An initial specimen will be introduced into the nutrient-filled source material. The specimen can be a cutting, seedling, germinating seed, or a small tree that is a suitable species for growing bonsais. Many species of trees are suitable for bonsai development and an enthusiast is able to choose from a variety of species, as long as the tree or shrub species is woody-stemmed, lives for longer than two years, is able to produce good branches, can be grown in a small pot to prune the roots.

Choosing the right type of bonsai is important because some trees are more difficult to maintain than others. Some bonsais require more sunlight than others and others may require more or less water. The best types of trees will be discussed in chapters to come, but it's important to choose a tree that you would like to tend to every day for the next several years. Even if you choose a slightly more difficult tree as a beginner, you can still successfully grow and nurture it if you give it enough time, love, and attention.

Whatever species you initially choose, especially if you are growing it from a seedling, you need to choose a bonsai that can be shaped to be relatively small throughout its lifetime and can meet all of the aesthetic standards that bonsai should meet. It's easy to grow a tree in a pot, but if it doesn't meet the aesthetic requirements of a full-grown tree, it starts to lose its point. One of the greatest visual factors of a bonsai is the fact that it looks like a miniature version of a large tree and becomes a living piece of art that you care for every day.

Because this is a piece of art, you want it to meet the specifications that you want. Of course, it is living and growing and it will change over time, but you will be able to change it according to the style that you like and you will be able to use a decorative pot that you like when you're planting your bonsai. You can choose multiple pots of different sizes as the tree grows but ensure that you choose one that is special to you to use when the tree is reaching its maximum size.

Find a place in your house that receives a fair amount of sunlight because most bonsai don't fare well with reflected light. In the Japanese tradition, it is practically unheard of to keep these trees indoors and they are usually kept outside in a protected area. But as bonsais have been adopted by more Western cultures, more people prefer to keep their bonsais indoors so they can watch them more regularly throughout the day. This makes it slightly more challenging to keep the tree healthy and it does take work, but this isn't impossible to accomplish.

The fundamental aspect of growing a bonsai is to do adequate research. As with starting any new hobby, it's necessary to find out which bonsai would be best suited to your environment, which one you like the look of, and which one you would like to nurture for years to come. The techniques that you will need to create a beautiful bonsai will all be discussed in the sections to come, but don't feel that you can't experiment with some of them. As part of the fundamentals of growing bonsai, it is a deeply personal experience, and you can adapt certain techniques according to how you want your piece of art to grow. The most important fundamental of bonsai growing is to love the entire process. There are going to be times that you may get frustrated or even impatient, but you will learn a lot about yourself during this process. It will help you find your inner peace if you allow it. There will be times you are going to be worried about your tree, especially when you prune the roots, but take it slow and treat it right and your bonsai will live for decades.

Before starting to describe the actual practical work, it is good to dwell a moment on some interesting distinctions that allow us to establish the first classification of bonsai.

It is important, in fact, to distinguish bonsai into two large groups:

Outdoor and indoor ones. The first are those who live in the open air without any particular damage. They usually belong to species accustomed to climates characterized by significant changes in temperature and sudden changes of season.

The latter, however, are those that need a moderate and constant temperature to survive. To these belong many tropical and subtropical species, such as ficus, schefflera, jacaranda, which would live very little if left exposed to our climates. Therefore, it is always good to read up on the needs and climatic habits of the plant, so as to offer it the best possible living condition.

Bonsai trees are also classified according to their height, which can vary from a minimum of 6 inches to a maximum of 47 inches. The "miniature" bonsai do not exceed the height of 6 inches. The "small" bonsai is less than 8.6 inches in size and are more readily available on the market. The "medium-small" bonsai reach the height of 16inches and for this, they are more easily cultivated. Then there are the "medium" bonsai that vary between 16 inches and 35 inches and the "large" ones, with a maximum height of 47 inches.

CHAPTER 2

How to Grow Bonsai

Those who are about to undertake the art of bonsai must keep in mind that it is a job that requires great attention and considerable patience, along with all the stages of development and growth of your bonsai, from the first moment of cutting the roots, the choice of the pot, the shape that the bonsai will have to take.

The beginner will not be able to immediately breed an excellent quality bonsai, but he will still be able to achieve many satisfactions managing to keep the size of the chosen tree or plant considerably reduced. The starting point of the work concerns the choice between the various ways to obtain a bonsai plant that meets our needs and abilities.

There are multiple ways that bonsai can be cultivated and some techniques are slightly more complicated than others, but given the right time and patience, all of these techniques can be performed by beginner enthusiasts. You might want to try your hand at a few of these methods once you fall in love with the whole process, but you may want to pick one of these methods first and then try it out.

There are many ways to get a map that can serve our purposes; among the most common, we will remember: Bonsai taken in nature, grown from seed, multiplied by cutting, multiplied by layering, obtained by grafting, bonsai purchased in a nursery. In this order, the main rules to be observed for the best results will be listed.

In this order, the main rules to be observed for best results will be listed.

Once you're confident with that method, move onto the next. This is a continuous learning process and you will discover something new about these little pieces of art every time you work with them.

RECOVERED IN NATURE OR YAMADORI

The Japanese translation for Yamadori means to collect small trees from a wild place like a forest. Sometimes trees can naturally remain small in nature because of a lack of sunlight, water, or nutrients in the soil. If two trees, for example, grow right next to each other, one's roots might grow faster and deeper allowing it to absorb more nutrients and water than its neighbor. This will allow its leaves and foliage to develop more quickly and it will start absorbing more sunlight. This will cast a shadow over its neighbor and then stunt its growth.

A rather easy way to get a plant is to take it directly in its natural environment: Going into a forest, it is often easy to find small plants that can meet our needs, requiring only the time of the pleasant walk.

Japan many bonsai, among the most famous for their beauty and seniority, like many black pines with five needles or junipers, were obtained with the Yamadori method.

However, not all the plants we encounter are suitable for becoming a bonsai, because, for various reasons, they would not grow in the right way, disappointing our expectations.

One of the best places to look in the wild for small trees that are advanced in years but still small in stature is close to larger trees that cast a shadow on them. Although it can be rather difficult to successfully dig out a small tree from the wild without over-damaging its root structure, these are the trees with some of the greatest and most unique bonsai properties. But digging up a tree may be illegal, so if this is something you want to do, you will need to first ascertain whether it is legal in that area and possibly get permission from the owner of the land.

The first thing to do, therefore, is to consider only plants that show themselves as the most robust and healthy, with small leaves, uniformly arranged on the branches.

It is good to make sure that the roots are also strong and well developed, and that the branches have grown in many directions, to give an impression of movement. Overall, the plant should look strong, small but compact.

Once the plant is chosen, the most delicate phase is that of transplanting, so it is good to pay close attention to how the operation is performed. The recommended period is just before spring when the vegetation awakens and the climate softens.

The roots defend themselves better from damage and are more willing to take root easily in new soil. However, good results were also achieved in late spring, between April and May, especially in mountain areas, and in autumn. Here's how it goes.

If you know that it's legal and you have the required permission, it's best to go out in the early months of spring to find a tree to dig up. Once you have found the tree that you think will make a suitable bonsai, then you should start digging around the tree carefully.

The soil around the tree is cleaned of blades of grass that hinder the work and those branches that will not serve our purpose or those that have grown excessively in length are cut, making the plant more manageable.

Dig a foot radius around the whole tree and also dig approximately a foot into the earth. It's important to take care that you don't overly damage the roots when you're digging. Ensure that when you cut through the roots, you do it as cleanly as possible, because roots that are overly bent and damaged will struggle to re-establish themselves later on and the tree will take the strain in its container.

Once the roots have carefully been severed, remove the tree from the earth and wrap the roots and remaining soil in moist towels to protect the roots while transportation. If the roots dry out, the tree will eventually die, so this is a necessary step and mustn't be skipped. It's important to note that the tree will be under stress while it's being transported and needs to be placed in a pot and re-soiled as soon as possible.

Any potting soil will suffice, but it must be nutrient-rich, so compost or diluted fertilizer should be included in the soil to help the roots after their trauma. If possible, it is ideal to include as much soil that the tree originally grew in into the pot because it's soil that the tree and the roots are already used to. This can be mixed in accordingly.

When preparing the pot, you need to use one that can drain well. A bonsai that receives too much water and can't get rid of the excess will not fare very well and may even die prematurely. Fill the pot with a mixture of soil and gravel to ensure adequate drainage and space for the roots to fit and grow into the container comfortably. (When making the soil mixture, ensure you use 50% soil and 50% gravel.)

If the plant is to be transported, the earth is sprayed with water and wrapped with damp gauze or newsprint, tying everything with twine in order to facilitate transport. It can be convenient to place the plant in a nylon bag that will also allow you to keep humidity constant. For a couple of months, waiting for the plant to resume all its functions, it is good to keep it in a normal pot with unfertilized soil, watering it abundantly and keeping it sheltered from wind and sun.

If the plant is to be transported, the earth is sprayed with water and wrapped with damp gauze or newsprint, tying everything with twine in order to facilitate transport. It can be convenient to place the plant in a nylon bag that will also allow you to keep humidity constant. For a couple of months, waiting for the plant to resume all its functions, it is good to keep it in a normal pot with unfertilized soil, watering it abundantly and keeping it sheltered from wind and sun.

A perforated transparent plastic bell is recommended to limit evaporation. When it begins to throw the first shoots,

then you can proceed with the repotting in a bonsai container.

Finally, gently unwrap the root system of the tree from the moist towel and place it in the pot. Once all of the roots are moved gently and comfortably placed, cover the soil/gravel mixture of the roots and pat down gently. It's best not to have the earth compacted because it will affect watering the roots.

Once the tree is securely planted, gently water it so as not to disturb the soil and the settling roots. The tree would be at risk at this point because its roots were damaged, so gentle care will be needed in the beginning stages. Watering heavily could disrupt the settling roots and harm the tree. After the bonsai has been watered, place it outside in a highly lit area, but keep it out of direct sunlight. A tree of this size probably isn't used to direct sunlight and it will dry out the soil much more quickly.

Keep the soil damp but never drenched, and leave the tree practically untouched for an entire year. If the bonsai is thriving after a year, then you can start styling it and considering repotting it if you need to. Additionally, it's necessary to occasionally include diluted fertilizers during the first year and especially in the summer months. The combination of warmth and nutrients will help the roots thrive. This will establish the tree and keep it healthy for years to come.

CULTIVATION FROM SEED OR MISHO

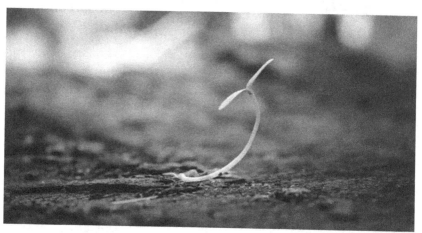

If you are the type of person who loves to start things from the very beginning and if you have the patience to enjoy this entire process, then the Misho method will be very satisfying.

This is the decidedly more fascinating method as it allows the seedling to grow and to follow its development from its seed state; however, it is also the method that takes the longest time before truly embarking on the art of bonsai. Sometimes there is talk of several years.

This method involves growing your bonsai from a tree seed of your choice and although it does take a very long time, you have a hands-on experience with the entire process. It will take a minimum of three years for a seedling to be mature enough to actually start shaping it into what you desire, but it does put you at an advantage because you have full control over your bonsai from the very beginning.

If this is the route that you would like to take, then there are several places where you can get tree seeds suitable for growing a bonsai. You can look in your surroundings or you can shop for some online. Do keep in mind that since bonsais are normal trees, they will come from normal tree seeds. There is no such thing as bonsai seeds and some people will try and sell these "bonsai tree seeds" at a much more expensive price, where in reality you could have probably found them outside for free.

If you do choose to look in your surroundings for tree seeds, then your future bonsai will be at an immediate advantage because if those types of trees are growing naturally in your area, then you are already in the perfect environment and climate for your bonsai to thrive.

Any locally sourced seeds should be planted as soon as fall begins for the best possible results. If you are interested in growing a foreign bonsai, it will be necessary to research exactly when it will be the best time to plant the seeds. If you are interested in planting seeds that come from a different region with a different climate, then you may need to employ a stratification technique to germinate the seeds.

The seeds can be found directly in nature, which implies a good one seed knowledge or purchased from a dealer. In both cases, it is important to bear in mind that some seeds need special care before they can be planted.

Some species must be subjected to a pre-germination period

in which the seeds are left for 24 hours in a basin full of water, the fertile seeds will deposit on the bottom forfeiting water, and the others will remain on the surface.

Other species must spend a cool period, between 2 and 8 degrees Celsius - 46.4 F., to be able to mature. In any case, it would be good to seek advice from a gardener who can adequately inform us about the needs of the various species of seeds.

As for seeds to buy, the packs on which the word Bonsai is written are preferred, even if any seed can become a good bonsai. But now, let's continue the job description.

After making the first decisions on the choice of seed, proceed with sowing.

The Stratification Technique

Stratification is the process of allowing seeds to germinate by simulating their natural growing conditions. Many tree seeds have the genetic programming to survive through the cold winter months in the ground and then start germinating in the spring. This enables them to maximize their chances of successfully growing into a tree and many tree seeds are only able to germinate after they've gone through a cold winter period. Therefore, if you are planting tree seeds out of season or from different climates, it may be needed to simulate a cold season to increase the likelihood of the seeds germinating. The majority of tree species will require you to soak the seeds in water before storing them in the refrigerator for a couple of months.   Some seeds require less time in a cold climate, whereas other species may require up to three months in the cold, so it will be necessary to research this before you begin the stratification process.

Planting the Seeds

The seedbed consisting of a small container filled with poor soil, which is without fertilizers (usually a mixture of sand and peat), is prepared. In this state, the seed is already in itself wrapped in sufficient nutrients to allow it to develop well.

The container should be filled up to 2 inches from the edge.

The initial preparation of your pot or container will be exactly the same for planting seeds as it would be for planting cuttings or a small tree. You will first apply a layer of coarse ground like gravel or lava rock at the bottom of the container to allow for adequate drainage. If seeds sit in soil that is too wet, it will cause them to rot and they won't be able to sprout.

Once you have added the soil layer on top of the coarse layer, you can start preparing your seeds. If your seeds need to be stratified, do this first, but if you have sourced local seeds and you are planting them at the right time, then you can forgo this process.

Once the moment of sowing has arrived (usually spring), proceed by burying the seeds with light pressure, the larger ones must be covered by at least 1inch of soil, the smaller ones by 0.5 inch.

If the size of the seed is really tiny then it will be sufficient to spread it regularly. We then begin to water them abundantly and gently, taking care not to create harmful grooves in the ground.

A solution with Chinosol can also be used.

Place the seeds in a container but ensure you leave at least two inches of space between each one. As the seeds continue to grow, they will require extra space for their roots to spread. And, if the roots intertwine you may end up damaging them when you try to re-pot the individual shoots. This can hurt the bonsai's progress.

Once the seeds are planted, another inch of bonsai soil must be added on top of the seeds and then gently compacted with your fingers. Once this is completed, water thoroughly and allow to drain. After that, don't water heavily again and only keep the soil moist until the seeds start to sprout.

Leave the seedlings alone for a year before you consider repotting. Performing this too early can put unnecessary strain on the root systems of the seedlings. Once they have been repotted, you must wait for at least another year before you consider shaping the bonsai. Even though this is a long process, it is still very satisfying to watch the little trees take form over this time.

At this point, it would be useful to cover the container with a glass or plastic bell, so as to keep the soil at a certain humidity and temperature (the ideal one is 18-20 degrees Celsius - 64.4-68 F.). The container should be kept away from the sun, often watering the soil to prevent the seeds from drying out. For this operation, the use of an inclined onion or a nebulizer is recommended, because, if the jet were too strong, it would move the earth and make the seeds float.

Once the seedlings are born, the bell can be removed and when the first leaves have sprouted, the transplant is carried out in a new container. It is important not to fertilize the land for at least a month.

After this period, the fertilizer will be administered in half the dose compared to that written on the pack. When the height of the seedlings will be 4 inches, you can begin to act on the shape.

MULTIPLICATION BY CUTTINGS OR SASHIKI

This method Sashiki consists of obtaining a new seedling using a part of an already formed plant. This allows us two main advantages:

First, we can easily dispose of a lot of bonsai material, simply by removing the parts of the plant that interest us.

Secondly, the multiplication by cutting allows us to maintain the same characteristics typical of the mother plant with absolute fidelity also for the following generations. However, even the cutting method while very easy to implement, is time-consuming. The cuttings are divided into four groups: It is possible to obtain a stem cutting, a sprouting cutting, a leaf-cutting and a root cutting.

The Sashiki method is one of the most popular and inexpensive ways for bonsai enthusiasts to propagate new trees because this process involves using tree cuttings. This method is much faster than trying to grow new trees through germinating seeds, and by using cuttings, the bonsai enthusiast can have more of an indication of some of the characteristics that the cutting will have if it starts to grow.

It is best to plan to gather tree cuttings in the spring and summer months when the trees are vibrant. Once you have decided which cuttings you would like (deciduous and conifer trees are normally the most successful), start gathering several cuttings. Look for healthy trees with healthy branches and make each cutting between two and four inches long. Additionally, look for branches that are only around an eighth of an inch thick, because they have greater success rates than thicker branches.

It's important to gather several cuttings at once because there is no guarantee that all of them will take root. Some of them may not be successful and if you only have one specimen, you may feel disheartened if it fails. But, if you have several specimens, the chances are greatly increased that one, or a few of them, will take root.

To ensure that the cuttings sprout roots, it's imperative to plant them in a substrate that will assist this process. In a small pot that can drain readily and easily, pour in a layer of a coarse draining substrate like gravel or lava rock. This substrate has no nutrients, but it helps the water drain far more quickly. Fill the container to around 1/3 of the way and then add a layer of bonsai soil. (Bonsai soil can be purchased at gardening shops and online and has a fair amount of nutrients, more than regular potting soil.)

But now we describe the simpler methods adopted:

Stem cutting: The stem cutting, also called eda-zashi, uses already fully mature and robust branches. These, if buried or immersed in water, develop their own root system, becoming autonomous plants. Therefore, branches not older than three years and which are not perishable due to disease or insects are to be chosen. Prune the cuttings at a 45-degree angle and place them into the soil about an inch deep. Once all of the cuttings are pushed into the soil, water the soil well and allow it to drain before putting it in a well-lit45-degree area.

After the initial heavy watering, keep the water moist and don't allow it to dry out. The nutrients from the soil will help the cuttings sprout roots and most should be successful. The branch must be around 8 inches long and must be cut immediately under a leaf node. The sprig must then be cleaned from the base by the leaves and planted in the ground, making sure that the shoots remain on the surface as much as needed.

After the cuttings have sprouted, plant them in individual little containers and allow them to grow. Cuttings are very successful ways of growing bonsais, but it will take several years before you will be able to shape them according to what you would like. But it's worth it and you won't be disappointed with this method. It must then be watered abundantly and covered with a glass or plastic plate.

It is important that during the first months the pot is in a bright place without being exposed to direct sun and that the soil is kept constantly humid. Once the first roots have sprouted, the seedling can be discovered from the slab and fertilized. Transplanting into a bonsai container should only be done once the roots are fully formed to develop.

Cutting from shoots: The cutting from shoots, called shinme-zashi, uses a young shoot to develop a new plant. The shoot must be cut obliquely with a sharp blade and must be leafless in the lowest part of its length. The other leaves, on the other hand, are simply to be checked by a third, so that evaporation is reduced to a minimum. Then the leafless stem of the bud is wrapped with a clay ball with a diameter of 1 inch, making sure that the lower part of the bud is positioned approximately in the center of the clay ball. You can finally proceed to bury the sprout up to completely cover the part wrapped in clay.

Leaf-cutting: Leaf-cutting, or ha-zashi, consists of planting a sprig in the soil leaving a leaf on the surface. The soil must be watered carefully and kept away from the sun. The sprig will emit the roots and develop other leaves.

Root cutting: The root cutting, called ne-zashi, consists instead of gathering the roots of the chosen tree during the winter season and cutting them into 3 inches long pieces. A container should be prepared to contain damp sand, on which the roots will be placed and left to rest until spring. Important, to cover the container with a glass plate and leave it at a temperature of 2-4 degrees Celsius – 35,6-39,2 F. When the roots begin to develop, transplanting can be carried out in suitable soil, making sure that the outermost part of the root is at ground level.

SPROUT CUTTING

LEAF CUTTING

ROOT CUTTING

MULTIPLICATION BY LAYERING OR TORIKI

This method of cultivating bonsais is slightly more challenging but it can still be performed by a beginner if they are up to a challenge.

The Toriki method works with air-layering and this allows for a tree or a branch of a tree to start forming new roots at a higher level because the nutrients of the existing root system have been interrupted. This sounds confusing, but sometimes a tree's trunk starts dividing into two, allowing two separate branches to grow.

Air-layering should always be done in the spring so the roots aren't exposed to extremes in temperatures and spring also maximizes the chances of roots sprouting.

This multiplication by layering consists of putting in contact a branch of the plant specially engraved with peat or earth, to make it root.

This is a method that allows you to obtain seedlings from rather large branches, in a short time, which would instead be very difficult to achieve by cutting.

The layering is recommended above all on some types of plants such as the Pomegranate, the Spruce, the Myrtle, the Maple, the Elm and the Cryptomeria, which have a great ability to develop roots both from the trunk and from the branches. It is preferable to undertake the operation in the spring, even if good results are obtained at any time of the year. Let's see how it goes together.

There are two different methods that can be used to air-layer a tree, namely the tourniquet method and the ring method. These methods are only used on trunks that are bifurcated and one that an enthusiast can remove one of the sections and grow a new bonsai from it.

The Ring: If you are more confident and believe that you will be able to grow the roots more quickly and cut away some bark without hurting the tree, the ring method may prove to be very successful.

Once the branch of the plant has been chosen, the lateral jets are removed for a short distance and engraved in the bark, forming a ring of about 1 inch in height around which the roots will form.

Two cuts from the bottom up to the sides of the branch can also be practiced, introducing a pebble or peat into the wound so that it does not close again.

There is also a third method of practicing the wound, consisting of wrapping two very close circles of wire tightly in the established point. In this way, with the growth of the tree, the wire will cut the bark gradually.

It is also important to sprinkle the wound with rooting hormone powder and prevent it from healing.

Layering Procedure

To obtain the roots, a transparent polyethylene sleeve stops under the incision, so as to create a funnel, and it is filled with peat to wrap the wound.

The sleeve is also closed over the incision with adhesive tape and the peat is constantly moistened. If the operation is unsuccessful, the branch will wither and die after a week or two; otherwise, the roots will begin to sprout.

When the root system is thick enough (usually 6-8 weeks), the new plant can be cut under the incision, placing it definitively in a container.

When the roots have well-rooted in the pot, you can proceed with the development of the bonsai.

Trees can be quite stubborn and they won't start sprouting roots until they are forced to do so. Thus, cutting a significant ring in the bark and including root hormone will force the tree to start sprouting roots in a place where it normally wouldn't. Once the wound has been dusted with root hormone, wrap it in wet sphagnum moss and then in plastic.

The Tourniquet: It's going to take some time and preparation to be confident enough to perform this method, but the first step is to wrap a piece of copper wire very tightly around the segment that you would like to cut off from the main trunk (preferably on one of the smaller off-shoots.) You should be able to use normal copper wire for this process, but if you have a bonsai with a thick trunk or a tree with a thick type of bark, you may need to use a copper wire with a thicker circumference.

Once you have tied the wire around the segment, it's important to sprinkle some rooting hormone over the damaged bark. This hormone, along with the lack of nutrients in the trunk, will cause roots to sprout quickly because the tree is going to try and survive the trauma. After the rooting hormone is added to the wound around the wire, wrap it with wet sphagnum moss and wrap it with plastic.

This method is less extreme than the ring method because it doesn't damage the bark as severely as the ring method but it does still sprout roots fairly quickly.

The Care for These Methods: Once the moss has been tied with plastic around the wounds, it is necessary to keep the moss moist at all times. It isn't advised to drench the moss because it will hinder the root growth, but keeping it moist will accelerate the growth of the roots. It will take a few months for the bag to fill with roots, but keep the stem attached to the main trunk during this process. Only when the bag is completely filled should you remove the stem with gentle cuts and plant the roots into fertile bonsai soil.

This method is tricky, but because you can remove a section of a bonsai that is already established, you will find that this will allow for rapid growth afterward; instead of waiting four or five years before you can start shaping the tree, it may be possible to start shaping the tree in around half the time.

PROPAGATION BY GRAFTING OR TSUGIKI

The Tsugiki method is also one of the more advanced methods and will take some practice, but just like the Toriki method, this method is also very rewarding. Translated from Japanese, Tsugiki means "to graft," and just like most other plant species, bonsais do thrive well with grafts.

Grafting two plants or trees together allows the strengths and characteristics of both plants to come through in their future development. This usually is beneficial to produce tastier fruits or more resilient plants, but grafting helps to add branches where needed and increase the foliage on a certain part of the tree. Some enthusiasts also try to combine the characteristics of two different trees that they like into one bonsai, but grafting is not an easy process and it can be risky. Without adequate practice, most grafts may be unsuccessful, so it's imperative to practice this technique on much cheaper plants and trees before you try it on a costly bonsai.

One of the most important principles of grafting is that you have to graft two trees between the same or a very similar species. Trees that are two different won't be compatible and the graft won't take. This won't only kill the graft, it might irreversibly damage the tree too. If you want to add to your bonsai, then you need to graft in branches of a species that is part of the same class or subclass.

Grafting is another way to get a bonsai plant. It consists of joining two different plants, to add their qualities into one. The plant on which the graft is practiced takes the name of "subject" or "portliness" (daiki), while the branch that is grafted is called "scion" or "grafting" (sugan: This process can be very useful for aesthetic purposes, to protect the plant from particular parasites, or to obtain a greater variety of fruit). In bonsai art, however, this method is often not recommended, especially the two types of grafting:

A) Basic grafting; B) Top grafting to beginners, due to the special care and experience it requires.

A

B

The grafting is generally practiced during the spring and with very young trees, of two or three years, which manage to adapt more easily to the various situations.

Now let's see how the two main types of grafting are made: The top ones and the base ones.

Top graft: Also called ten-tsugi or Scion grafting, is made in the upper part of a plant. It is the most common sort of grafting, and it involves removing a small branch or shoot from a larger donor plant and then inserting it into another plant. With this type of graft, the end of the shoot is cut at a 45-degree angle and then a similar groove is made into the receiving plant, so the shoot can fit snugly into the groove.

This technique is commonly used with juniper and pine trees, but most deciduous and evergreen trees cope very well with this type of grafting. If you have a bonsai of one of these species, you can use this grafting method to easily add extra branches or include extra foliage on the top of the tree. (The leaves on top of bonsais can seem rather sparse, so this is a way to make your bonsai seem fuller and allow for a richer look.) When these grafts are done carefully and they fit well in the beginning, there will be a little-to-no indication that there ever was a graft performed.

It is absolutely necessary to ensure that both the donor and the receiver are both in good health. If one of the trees is in ill health, the graft won't be successful, and if there is an infection in the graft, there is a small risk of spreading it to the receiving tree. Always ensure that both trees have healthy foliage and seem very similar in stature before grafting. One of the best ways to ensure that both trees are healthy is to fertilize both trees well in the season before you are going to graft. Since grafting is best performed in early spring, it's best to fertilize regularly throughout the spring and summer months the year prior.

It's also best to protect both trees during the winter months. Frost and snow (if you are working with larger trees) can severely damage the branches and make them less likely to be grafted together. Thus, it's best to cover the branches that you want to use for grafting (it might not be possible to cover the whole tree if the tree is large, but it is possible with most bonsais).

Once you're ready to start grafting in early spring, identify which shoots you believe are most likely to join with each other. It's ideal to look for shoots that have a strong woody base and are at least 2 ½ to 4 inches long and around a ¼ inch in diameter. Don't look for any branches that are too thick because the thinner ones have a more flexible interior and have a higher probability of joining properly.

It's necessary to clean a sharp grafting knife with alcohol before cutting a shoot from the donor tree and then re-cleaning the knife before making the groove into the receiver. It may seem strange to go to this extent, but sterilizing the blade with alcohol lowers the risk of any parasites being spread between the trees.

Cut the scion with one long stroke at an angle to create a sharp point to move into the groove of the receiving tree. Since you have gone through the trouble of cleaning your knife, do not touch the cut end of the shoot with your bare hands. Contaminating the end can lessen the likelihood of acceptance.

Once you place the shoot into the receiving tree (do this as smoothly as possible as not to hurt the wood), use grafting tape to secure the branch. Wrap it around the area that you have cut and treat it like you would treat an injury on a person. Don't tie the tape too tightly because it can cut off the nutrients into the branch, but don't leave it too loose because it comes undone and the branch may not stay secured.

Ensure that the wrapping is sufficient enough to prevent water from seeping into the graft. Unlike other planting methods, you want to avoid having water seep into any graft because it can create the shoots and the scions to start to rot. You can add some plastic wrap around the tape to help with this if you are concerned about moisture or rain.

Leave the dressing on the graft throughout the winter months and watch for any new signs of life in the spring. Any new sprouts, shoots, or flowers are indicative that the graft was successful. If you see that this is starting to occur, you can slowly unwrap the dressing around the graft because the tree would have healed at this point.

Basic graft. The basic graft, or moto-tsugi, concerns instead a lateral union that is practiced at the base of the trunk or branch of a plant.

In this case, we proceed in a slightly different way: The cut of the rootstock must be practiced literally from top to bottom for the depth of about 1 inch, creating a sort of notch in the trunk.

The cut of the scion must then be studied in an appropriate

way to this notch, so as to fit perfectly into the rootstock, allowing quick healing of the wound.

Also, in this case, a strong binding will be necessary to facilitate the union of the two parts. Before transplanting it is good to cut the leaves in half and cut the main root.

This will assist in welding, limiting the growth of the rootstock.

Once practiced any of the two grafts it is good to place the plant in a place sheltered from the sun and drafts, watering to keep the soil moist, but without exceeding, so as not to rot the roots. After a month, the graft should begin to throw new shoots, then the binding must be eliminated and the soil fertilized in small doses.

However, the following factors should always be kept in mind.

Plants must be compatible: It is not possible to graft two plants that have too different characteristics, such as an apple tree and an orange.

The part of the two plants that come into contact, called the change, must be carefully joined because nourishment passes from it to the upper plant. Never practice grafting in an unsuitable season, such as winter.

The direction of the buds of the scion must be the same as that of the rootstock, i.e., upwards.

A bonsai obtained by grafting, however, can begin to show good results only after a couple of years of careful care.

NURSERY BONSAI

Buying the plant in a nursery is certainly the easiest way to start a bonsai, as it does not involve any of the risks mentioned above. However, it excludes the great satisfaction of growing a bonsai from the early stages. It is very important, however, to carefully consider the plant you want to buy; it is easy, to come across rather expensive specimens that deserve careful consideration.

In order not to incur unpleasant accidents, we list the three main evaluation criteria of a bonsai, so that we can get an idea of the appropriate price:

When you are about to buy a Bonsai, you have to consider some aspects to make your purchase valuable and worthy.

Preferably, contact shops or garden centers of a certain level and reliability, managed by trained personnel who can help you in case of difficulty.

Do not focus on a certain type of essence, that is a certain variety of tree: choose an essence that is easy to care for, that can survive in your environment and climate, even if the plant is a little less beautiful than the one you wanted; after gaining more experience you will be able to grow more beautiful and challenging plants. The first characteristic is the age: The older a bonsai is, the higher its price will rise. However, it is well known that age is often increased during the purchase phase. We recommend giving importance to age, but above all to focus on the aesthetic aspect of the plant we want to buy.

The general aspect of the bonsai is also important and must be healthy and vigorous.

During the purchase, therefore, it is necessary to consider the state of health and robustness of the tree, starting from the root system which must have well-developed rootlets, up to the branches and crown which must be proportionate and harmonious. In this regard, it is good to know that if the bonsai has visible wounds; these do not diminish the value of the plant.

The important thing is that they are well healed and that they do not aesthetically ruin the general appearance.

The bonsai must have a simple shape, which respects the basic styles of which we will talk shortly.

It is therefore advisable to decide to buy the tree when you already have in mind the main characteristics that you want in bonsai, according to the style and species you have chosen.

Observe the leaves of the tree you decide to buy: from April to late September the leaves must be a beautiful deep green, with no brown spots or crumpled parts. Moreover, the tree must not have leafless branches, unless it is made on purpose: in this case, you would recognize them because they are also without bark and are called JIN.

In autumn and winter, this is slightly more difficult due to the lack of leaves on many species. In this case, we must rely on the fairness of the seller.

Look and gently touch the earth inside the vase: it must not show cracks and must not be detached from the edge of the vase, and it must be compact (but not as hard as a brick). Avoid plants buried in pure clay, which you can recognize by touching it since it feels like plasticine. In short, the earth must be compact and porous to allow both water and air to pass properly.

If there is moss it should be soft and without dry spots, this would indicate that the plant has not been kept in ideal humidity conditions.

If the earth is pressed into the pot, water comes out as from a sponge, just leave it: most likely the plant will last very little.

Look at the branches of the Bonsai: if you notice some iron wire (which is aluminum) planted in the bark, do not buy the plant, if it survives it will be ruined forever.

Considering these criteria, we will be able to assess whether or not the price of a bonsai corresponds to its main characteristics.

GIFTED BONSAI

If we receive the Bonsai as a gift, the first thing to do is to find out what species the Bonsai is. If the plant was bought in a garden center, there will be a tag indicating its species.

If there is no tag, read up and try to find out which variety the Bonsai belongs to in order to have at least useful information on how to handle it.

Let's look at the foliage, if present, since it could be winter; if in the middle of the vegetation there are dry branches with bark still attached, let's get a pair of scissors and remove them.

If the branches are dry but white and peeled, leave them: they were made on purpose.

If the gift arrives during spring or summer, let's remove the dry foliage too, if present.

Unfortunately, it could happen that the earth in the pot is not of the right type, so we will water it and, as soon as the earth has created a "brick effect", that is when it has become very hard and no longer absorbs water, repot the plant. Repotting the plant is an extremely complicated operation to perform.

Look at the branches of the Bonsai: if they are wrapped in aluminum wire, check that this is not planted in the wood. If, on the contrary, the thread is penetrating the branches, remove it.

HOW TO ATTACH BONSAI TO YOUR CONTAINER

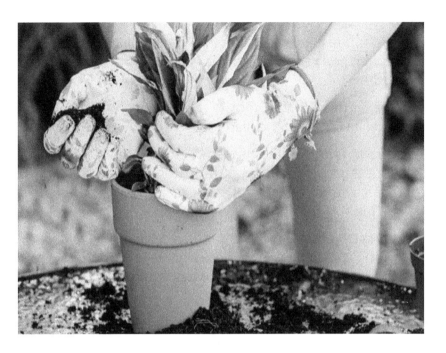

Given the size and small thickness of many bonsai containers, there is often the risk that the plant will not be able to stand alone. It is therefore necessary to anchor it to have greater support.

There are two anchoring methods: The roots of the tree are stopped using metal wire at the bottom of the container.

This can be done in two ways: Either by tying the wire to the drainage metal mesh or by letting the wire come out of the drain hole and then stopping it under the pot.

In the case of group bonsai, only the largest trees will be anchored to the container, then tying to those smaller ones. Threads will be removed when the roots have developed sufficiently.

On the one hand, a moist mixture of potting soil and peat is prepared and wrapped, compressing it, around the roots of the tree, to weigh it down and make it more stable. It then ends by filling the container with normal soil.

We will now deal with that part of the bonsai care that concerns transplanting, that is moving the plant from one soil to another, and repotting, that is, moving from one container to another,

Transplanting has the utility of providing new fertile soil and chemical balanced to the plant.

The earth is gradually depleted by the tree that uses mineral substances as nourishment. It is therefore necessary to replace it with new soil to prevent the plant from weakening or wasting.

The main purpose of the repotting instead is to limit the size of the roots, favoring the development of rootlets which, although small in size, provide most of the nourishment to the plant.

For each repotting, therefore, you can use a smaller pot, or at the maximum keep the size of the previous pot. However, it is good to prepare the container, sterilizing it from germs, and cover it.

I give the drainage holes with a thin mesh metal mesh, so as to allow the water to pass without the soil coming out.

If the container is very high, a drainage layer of about 1inch must be created using pebbles.

This will allow the water not to stagnate. It should be remembered that the right period for repotting is the beginning of spring, except for tropical and subtropical plants which can be repotted at any time of the year.

Besides, young plants must be repotted every year, to accompany their rapid growth, while the older ones can wait even two or three years. It is however good to note that the plant needs repotting when the soil rises above the edge of the container due to the thrust that the roots provide. Repotting should be started when the soil is dry, so you can work more easily. Here's how it goes.

You turn the pot upside down and, holding the bonsai by the trunk, hit the bottom of the container so as to gently let the soil out with the roots.

After bringing the bonsai back in the right direction, proceed to clean the roots of the residual earth and shorten those too long by a third. The main root, the larger one, will be checked and dead or too weak roots will be eliminated.

After pruning, the container is filled with a thin layer of soil and the bonsai is placed in the pot, taking the measures for a correct arrangement: The root of the roots must not exceed the edge of the pot.

Pour more soil into the container without exceeding, pressing it to make it adhere well to the root system, and proceed with watering, taking care not to create grooves in the ground, and placing the pot in a sheltered place.

However, it is recommended not to use the fertilizer for at least one or two months after repotting.

It is good now to spend a few words about the ideal soil for bonsai, so as to provide each plant with the best nutritional intake and the best possibility of development.

The most suitable soil is absolutely the original one of the plants, although none is always easy to dispose of.

Therefore, different types of soil must be purchased to have a suitable mixture.

Application of metal mesh for drainage

Drainage in a tall container with wire mesh and pebbles

In case you already have available the earth and you run the risk that contains insect eggs, you will have to spread it in the sun so that the eggs die.

You can also sterilize the earth with fingers or chloropicrin.

Bonsai soil is a mixture of various elements, such as peat, sand and clay. Each of these elements gives the soil certain characteristics, the clay is the actual greasy soil, and the peat provides the humus while the sand allows the soil to breathe more easily and chooses water.

However, each plant has certain needs, due to the speed of growth, the need for humidity, and above all the degree of acidity of the soil.

Acidity is a very important element for the good development of the plant, therefore, it must be carefully observed. We recommend the purchase of a pH-meter, of the mixture, so as to offer the best soil to the plant.

A large quantity of plants prefers an acidity degree between 5.5 and 6 on the pH meter scale.

We can schematize the degree of acidity necessary for the various plants in this way: Device for measuring acidity;

-        PH less than 3.7: Plants that grow in areas with acidic soil.

-        PH between 3.8 and 4.5: Spruce, Canadian fir, birch and poplar.

-        PH between 4.6 and 5.5: Most conifers.

-        PH between 5.6 and 6.9: Almost all deciduous trees.

-        PH between 7.0 and 8.0: Plants that live in neutral or alkaline grasslands.

If there are imbalances between the plant and the soil, the mixture must be modified, adding a lot of peat, a very acidic substance, if we want to increase the acidity degree, or removing it, if we want to decrease it, possibly adding lime or calcium carbonate, so as to correct it further.

However, general rules can be laid down on the composition of the mixture for some plants. For example, young plants, or in general deciduous that have rather rapid growth, need more oily soil, therefore a mixture consisting of 1/3 of clay, 1/3 of peat, and 1/3 0 sand is recommended. Slow-growing plants, like conifers, need more sandy soil, so the mixture should be 1/4 clay, 1/4 peat 2/4 sand. However, it is good to sift the final mixture in order to and the soil agglomerates, making it uniform and homogeneous.

After filling the container, it is good practice to also apply the last layer of pulverized moss or leaf soil mixed with soil to give a more natural and wilder image to the creation

It is absolutely necessary to change your bonsai's pot every few years, because if a bonsai becomes pot--bound, it will deplete all the nutrients in the soil, and it will inevitably die. A tree that doesn't have its pot changed can't allow its roots to grow further, and the growth will be completely stunted. Transplanting and repotting your bonsai allows it more space and nutrients to grow and flourish.

Even though it's necessary to repot your bonsai, it won't be a regular occurrence. Even the fastest-growing trees are only repotted every couple of years and more mature trees are only repotted every three to five years. Repotting isn't something that is routine and it is something that you can judge subjectively according to your tree. You can judge this by gently removing your tree from its pot in the early months of spring and see if there are roots encircling the entire root system. If this is the case, then the bonsai needs to be repotted into a larger container before the roots strangle themselves.

The best time to repot your bonsai is in early spring because the tree is still dormant after the winter months. This is important because the tree isn't supporting foliage at this point, so if any roots are accidentally damaged during the transfer, it shouldn't cause any permanent or severe problems with your bonsai.

You can choose any style of pot for your bonsai, as long as it's large enough to comfortably house all the roots.

For this topic we have written a separate chapter in order to choose the best vase also for aesthetic reasons. Before you repot your bonsai, ensure that you have all the necessary tools for a smooth transfer. The tools you will need for this process are a small root rake, sharp scissors for pruning, a chopstick, and a wire cutter.

If you have bought a bonsai that is already grown and

potted, many sellers will anchor the tree to the pot they're planted in, and it will be necessary to cut the anchoring wire at the drainage holes to prevent you from hurting your tree when you try to remove it.

Once this is completed, carefully lift the entire ground and root mixture out of the pot using the root rake and check the root development within the pot. If the roots are still sparse and not encircling each other, you can return the tree to its original pot for another year and recheck it the following spring, but if you notice the roots are becoming cramped in the small pot, then it will be time to repot your bonsai.

Before moving the tree to its new pot, take the time to scrape away the old soil from the roots with a chopstick. This will allow new, nutrient-filled soil to take up that space to feed the bonsai in the new pot. Try your best not to damage the roots during this process, so don't rush cleaning the roots. It is important to note that if you have a pine bonsai that you chose to grow, you must keep at least half of the old soil attached to the roots because the roots grow mycorrhizal fungus and this helps nourish and protect the tree.

After you have removed the adequate amount of dirt from the roots, grab your scissors and start pruning any roots that have grown too long, but don't ever prune more than 30% of the total roots. This will cause too much trauma to the tree and the tree will have a high likelihood of dying. So, proceed with caution with this step.

Build your new pot with fine mesh over the drainage holes and fill it with the usual drainage mix and then some bonsai soil before adding the tree. Top it up with more bonsai soil until the pot is filled and press the soil down gently with your fingers. You can add a few pebbles on the top of the soil because it helps guide water and it improves the decoration of the piece itself.

Finally, water the tree thoroughly and then keep the soil moist thereafter.

CHAPTER 3

Bonsai and Its Styles

Since bonsais are living works of art and because no tree is going to grow quite like another, they all have unique traits, and these traits can be manipulated according to what you would like your bonsai to look like.

Styling your bonsai is one of the most enjoyable parts of keeping these beautiful trees and although there are many styling methods, they are open to the interpretation of the individual. There are guidelines that one can follow to help style their bonsai, but because trees are all unique, they can change according to their normal growth patterns and how you manipulate them.

Once the bonsai has found its definitive seat in the pot, you can devote yourself to the development of the aerial part of the plant.

To do this, bonsai requires continuous attention, ranging from pruning, topping, to the application of metal wire, etc. All these operations contribute to giving the bonsai a particular shape. In fact, in bonsai practice, there are many traditional styles that condition the shape of the crown, of the stem, and the branches of the tree according to specific rules.

Starting from the assumption that a bonsai is in all respects a miniature tree and that therefore has its own aesthetic harmony; the styles derive their reason of being from the careful observation and cataloging of the forms of their corresponding "giant cousins."

The bonsai artist tries in a few words to reproduce at bonsai level all those forms that over time nature has produced in normal trees. Therefore, below we will cover the main styles that regulate the forms of bonsai single or in groups. Before choosing one, however, it is good to look at the plant we have available, looking at it from the height of the pot and not from above, and trying to identify which style best suits its structure. We are now going to consider all the bonsai styles that are suitable for a single plant. We will describe: Hokidachi; Chokkan; Moyogi; Shakan; Kengai; Han-Kengai; and that of the twisted trunk.

SINGLE STYLES

Hokidachi style- Hokidachi styling is known as the broom method because the trees are grown remarkably straight with a thick base that gently narrows towards the top. This style is best suited for deciduous trees that have fine branches. The trunk is grown absolutely straight but it doesn't extend all of the way to the top of the tree. Instead, the fine branches grow around the top of the tree and give it a "broomy" look. These branches are pruned to grow around the top third of the tree and this allows leaves, flowers, and even little fruits to decorate the top of the tree.

This style is common amongst beginners because, with the correct support, an enthusiast can guide the trunk of the tree to grow absolutely straight. Other styles require a lot of manipulation where this style requires a straight support next to the stem as it matures. After the tree is matured, the pruning will be simple enough to keep in this style. This is a beautiful and simple style for both beginners and experts.

Chokkan or erect style- The Chokkan style has a completely straight tree, with the strongest and thickest branches growing to a third of its height and thinning more and more going upwards.

The Chokkan style is also very common amongst beginner enthusiasts because it has a straight trunk. It is a style that many trees have in nature, especially if a tree is exposed to a lot of light and doesn't face competition from trees too close together.

The Chokkan is similar to the broom style, but unlike the broom style, this trunk starts thick at the bottom and tapers out as it approaches the top. This is the usual styling of pine trees in nature, and pine bonsais look very similar as they do on a much larger scale. The branches and foliage should be pruned to start growing from as low as a quarter way up from the soil.The branches are arranged symmetrically with respect to the trunk and gradually shorten, giving the tree the image of a cone.

As already mentioned, since the branches must always grow parallel to the ground, it is good to apply the metal wire, if necessary. Conifers are the plants that respond most to this style.

These types of bonsai are particularly beautiful and can be pruned easily. This is one of the best types of bonsai for beginners.

Moyogi or curved trunk style - It is a rather simple style to take care of as it is very natural for the tree. The bonsai has a very balanced shape as the trunk grows straight upwards with some slight curvatures. The branches grow randomly outside the curvatures and gradually thinner to the top.

The most suitable plants for this style are oaks, beeches and maples.

The Moyogi style is the informal upright style of bonsai that is also readily found in nature. These types of trunks are normally formed in an "S" shape and branches shoot out from each bend. This trunk also starts with a thick base and then tapers out close to the top and grows thick foliage on the top of the tree. This type of bonsai is a prime candidate to accept grafts if the foliage is too thin on the top of the tree.

This type of style can be manipulated but many bonsais,

especially ficus and some deciduous trees, will grow naturally into this type of shape if left to their own growth patterns. Pruning will tend to give this shape to the tree, especially eliminating the larger branches that grow towards the top of the plant.

This style is easy to grow and it's easy to maintain, but it is also beautiful to look at and practically all bonsai enthusiasts are happy with this type of style.

Shakan or sloping trunk style – This style of bonsai is slightly more advanced than the previous three and it occurs in nature when winds blow dominantly in one direction forcing the trees to grow in a particular direction. Trees in valleys and on the sides of mountains are prone to grow like this because wind can be forced down the gradients. The trunk of the bonsai in this case is no longer upright, but tilted diagonally, forming one or more angles with respect to the ground. The branches grow in all directions and always horizontally.

Characteristic of this style is that the superficial roots protrude from the ground and follow the direction in which the plant inclines.

If an enthusiast wishes to grow their bonsai in this type of style, they would have to ensure that the tree grows at an angle of between 60 and 80 degrees relative to the ground they're planted in. The roots of these types of trees are slightly different from other bonsai, and they will need to be pruned accordingly. The roots on the side opposite to the angle need to be stronger and heavier than the other side of the container, so the weight of the tree can be supported.

When pruning this type of bonsai, it's necessary to ensure that the first branch on the tree is on the opposite side to the tilt, as to work as a form of counter-balance. The image above doesn't have this because the initial trunk is still vertical before the tilt sets in. If the tilt starts from the base, then it's imperative to have a large branch grow off early on to help the tree stay balanced.

This is a more challenging style to grow, but it is a beautiful addition to any enthusiast's collection.

Kengai or waterfall style - This style reproduces the arrangement of those trees that for natural causes have grown in particularly steep places.

The trunk, therefore, bends strongly downwards, coming out of the container, giving the impression of a cascade of leaves. It is important to use a rather tall container, to allow the tree to come out as much as possible, to accentuate the effect more.

Some trees grow on the sides of cliffs but to maintain their balance naturally, some trees grow down and instead of up. The trees germinate and sprout on the cliff and start growing towards the light, but as soon as the tree starts to get heavier, it can't maintain its weight and then starts to grow downward.

Because these trees normally grow on rocks, the availability of nutrients is greatly reduced and the trees don't grow excessively large. After seeing these types of trees in the wild, the Japanese were very interested in growing them for themselves.

This is definitely one of the more difficult styles that you can choose to try and shape your bonsai into because it is unnatural for trees to grow downward. It requires a solid root system and strong but gentle support throughout the entire growth process. This bonsai also requires enough height that it can continue to grow downward, but you have to ensure that it doesn't become too heavy and put excessive weight on the root system.

Kengai, or cascading, bonsai need tall pots and, even though the tree will be grown upright for a while, it will have to be bent into a downward position before the trunk becomes too strong. The flexibility of a young tree (between two and three years) is adequate to safely move into a downward position and continue its growth pattern from there. It may become too risky to move a tree into that type of position after this period because there is a risk of cracking and splintering the trunk. If this happens, the tree will most likely die.

This is an unusual form of bonsai and is one of the more advanced styles, but it is still worth attempting because the results are mesmerizing.

The plants most indicate are conifers and azalea.

Han-Kengai or half-cascade style - This style is very similar to the previous one, except that the trunk comes out of the pot but stays at the edge. The branches are arranged in such a way as to lean slightly downwards, as soon as they come out of the edge, to straighten upwards, immediately afterward. The trees suitable for this style are those of the previous one.

Twisted-trunk style - It is a style that gives a very similar look to the Chokkan one. Also in this case the branches are thinned and shortened towards the top, making the trunk, however, twists on itself, losing to the branches that symmetry that characterizes the Chokkan.

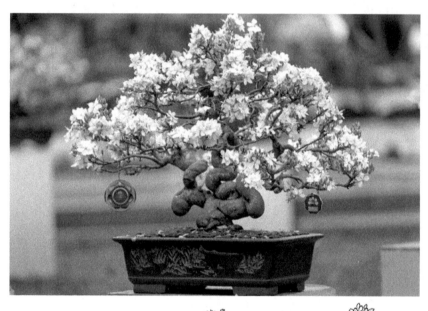

1)Chokkan;

2)Moyogi;

3)Shakan;

4)Kengai;

5)Han-Kengai;

6) Twisted trunk style

GROUP STYLES

Growing bonsai can be rather addictive and as you become more and more confident with certain skills, you might feel like you would like to expand your expertise to a greater level. Having group styles and more than one tree in one container is a great way to start moving into more advanced levels.

Let's now consider those styles that are suitable for groups of bonsai, both those grown from the same root, and those grouped together. According to Japanese bonsai rules, there should never be a pan number of plants, except for number two.

Sokan or style of the twin trunks- The double and triple-trunk feature (Sokan and Sankan) is common in trees in nature, but it is rather rare to see it as a bonsai.

This style concerns two trees grown from the same root.

It happens for trunks that sprout from the same root system, but because of the confined space, it is rare for bonsai to be able to do this. But when this does happen, the two or three or trunks will vary in length, thickness, and how many branches they produce.

The thicker and most developed trunk will grow upright with one or two other trunks growing outward, but all of the trunks will contribute toward the foliage to make a complete canopy in the years to come.

This isn't necessarily a technique that one can force onto their bonsai and although it can happen naturally, it will require a few extra precautions when repotting these types of bonsais. The roots may intertwine and be very delicate closer to the trunks and damaging them may irreversibly hurt the tree. Thus, take extra care when dealing with these types of bonsai.

The tree that has a more robust trunk is usually called the father, the other son.

The point where the two trees join the root must be as low as possible, so as to give the impression that the bonsai is a composition of two completely autonomous plants.

Sankan or triple trunk style - This style is a variant of the previous one since three twin trees branch off from the root, which must have different sizes to recognize a father, the largest, the son, the minor, and the mother, the one intermediate. Again, the conjunction with the root should be as low as possible.

Kabudachi or multiple trunk styles – The Kabadachi style is very similar to Sokan and Sankan because it refers to a tree with multiple trunks but they all come from the same root system. Yose-ue, on the other hand, is slightly different because it is the forest form of bonsai collections.

This is arguably one of the most complicated and advanced forms of keeping bonsai because it not only takes patience, it also takes a remarkably gentle hand and significant experience. In these designs, the larger trees are arranged in the middle of the display with the smaller ones on the outskirts to resemble a real forest. These can be grown from seedlings and nurtured and styled in the same container, or you can move more mature trees into one display. But caution is needed here because the roots of the trees will intertwine and they will be easily damaged. Thus, you will need the help of a few people if you ever had to move the forest bonsai into a larger container so the roots aren't overly damaged.

Always starting as a base from the Sokan, in this style trees are left to grow from the roots in any odd number greater than three, so as to form a small forest.

It is also necessary to remember for this style the importance of the conjunction of plants with roots.

Ikadabuchi or raft style - According to this style, the tree looks like it has fallen to one side and has begun to root downwards and branch upwards, creating new stems that arise from the ground.

For this style, it is better to choose a plant with many branches on one side of the trunk, by cutting or directing the other branches in the right way.

The main trunk must be arranged horizontally and partially covered with earth, making all the branches come out vertically.

As the months go by, new roots will grow in the lower part of the trunk and it will become necessary to cut the original roots of the tree which, until then, were arranged horizontally.

There are also options of growing groups of bonsai on larger pieces of wood, which is known as the raft bonsai style or Ikadabuki. This method is effective because either the wood will start to degrade and give extra nutrients to the bonsai, or the bonsai will find the roots of the wood and start joining their roots with theirs. The conjoining of roots allows for multiple bonsai to grow together with the piece of wood. This method is very successful in group styles because it is less likely for the bonsai to lack nutrients, unlike in rocky terrains, which are far riskier.

Group styles are normally more advanced, but there is no reason for you not to try your hand at some of these styles. Once your confidence has grown in managing single bonsais, you will manage group styles fairly easily.

Netsuranari or sinuous raft style - It is a style that derives from the previous one, from which it differs only for a small feature.

In fact, the trunk of the tree, always arranged horizontally, twists on itself, giving the whole bonsai a sinuous effect.

Yose-ue or forest style -The Yose-ue style refers to the composition of several trees of the same species, but of different ages and sizes, so as to form a miniature forest.

This style requires special preparation and care as, for a good aesthetic result, both spaces and the arrangement of plants must be carefully dosed.

However, it is possible to define some rules that facilitate the composition.

-       First of all, it is good to keep in mind already from which angle you want the bonsai to be observed.

It is therefore recommended to prepare an approximate drawing of the desired arrangement, so as to study the way to prevent two plants from being covered by each other.

- Usually, the trees are arranged in decreasing order of height: In the foreground the larger ones, the medium ones in the center, and at the bottom the smaller ones.

This is to give the overall composition a greater three-dimensional effect.

- Always keep in mind that even the empty spaces between the trees have great importance for the harmony of the image.

Great importance also assumes the preparation of the pot in which the bonsai will be planted. This must have a narrow edge and be elongated in shape, large enough to allow each tree adequate root space.

On the bottom of the container, it is necessary to place a wire mesh with tight links, carefully covered with the first layer of gravel and a subsequent layer of bonsai soil.

After arranging the trees, add more soil to the empty spaces and press it carefully.

BOTH SINGLE AND GROUP BONSAI STYLES

We will now see the styles that are suitable for both single and group bonsai.

Hokidachi or inverted broom style- The Hokidachi gives the bonsai an appearance reminiscent of an inverted broom, with the branches starting just above the middle of the stem and fan-shaped upwards until reaching the top. The trunk is erect.

The roots must also be thick and robust and distributed harmoniously in the soil.

A tree suitable for this style, however, is not easy to find in nature, therefore the use of metal wire or even the entire development process from cuttings or by layering is recommended so that the desired shape can be reached more precisely.

Fukinagashi or windswept style - It is a style that requires a lot of care to get good results.

It is rather similar to the Shakan, with the trunk inclined diagonally, with the difference that its branches are not arranged on both sides of the trunk, but extend only on the inclination side, so as to give the impression that the tree is prey to the continuous force of the wind.

It is therefore necessary to cut all the branches that grow on the opposite side to the inclination and let the others thicken and grow stronger.

The branches must always develop horizontally. Even the roots, to respect the image of the tree that fights against the wind, must be very robust and well planted in the ground.

1) Sokan, 2) Sankan, 3) Kabudachi, 4) Ikadabuchi, 5) Netsuranari, 6) Yose-ve

Bunjingi or littered style - This style gives greater importance to the trend of the trunk than to the crown. The bonsai, in fact, is completely bare of branches along the entire length of the stem, except on the top, where small branches develop.

The trunk can be totally erect or have more or less pronounced inclinations, but always so as to maintain a certain harmony of form.

ISHITSUKI OR ROCKY STYLE

Ishitsuki is one of the most fascinating styles of bonsai art, as it requires a certain capacity, in addition to offering a remarkable aesthetic effect. It is called a rock style because inside the container a rock of variable size is placed, which can have two main functions: Either to be simple support for the roots (Ishitsuki on rock) or to be the place where the roots are rooted (Ishitsuki in the rock).

It is good to use rocks that have strong angles and bright colors in order to give a vital image to the composition.

In the event that a rock does not fully satisfy us from the point of view of the shape, it is possible to work with a chisel to bring it closer to our desires.

As for the containers, the oval ones are shallow, with colors and dimensions in harmony with the structure of the rock and the bonsai. However, the containers usually have neutral colors to counterbalance the more vivid ones of the rock.

Before starting the real work, it is good, also in this case, to make some preliminary sketches to get an idea of how the final composition will look, studying both the point of view from which the bonsai will be observed, both the natural situation and possibly you want to recreate.

It will also be useful to guarantee the bonsai a long and robust root system so that it easily adapts to the new environment in which it will live.

An easy method is to plant the tree in a very deep container and root it well. Every 3 months 1inch of soil will be removed from the surface of the pot, while keeping the plant at the original height, in order to leave the roots in the open air and to force them to stretch to look for the nourishment in the soil below, The operation will be repeated until the roots have reached a satisfactory length and the plant will then be ready to become a good rocky bonsai.

Now we will examine the differences between the two cases and show how to make a good rocky bonsai.

Ishitsuki on rock – According to this style, the tree is placed on the top of a medium-small rock with the roots that run along with it until it is planted in the ground, giving the impression of wanting to imprison it. It is, therefore, necessary to choose a tree that has robust roots and arranged in a sunburst pattern and, once placed on the rock, it will contribute to the harmony of the image by cutting the roots too large or too thin.

The tips of the roots are buried in the ground and the others are stopped at the rock to ensure greater stability for the plant.

To do this, it is recommended to use either tape or a metal wire which will be blocked as much as possible inside the cavities of the rock.

After the arrangement, these roots are covered first with a mixture of clay and peat for the thickness of 1 inch, then with the soil wrapped with muslin bandages, it is good to water abundantly and repeatedly, keeping this layer of the soil always moist. In fact, the plant has a great need for nourishment, since the roots are only partially in contact with the earth.

After about 5 months, or in any case, when the roots are sufficiently developed in the pot, muslin and layer of soil on the rock can be eliminated.

From now on the tree is ready to become a good bonsai.

Ishitsuki in the rock- As for Ishitsuki in the rock, the tree is arranged so that the roots penetrate small cavities and root them. The rock will, therefore, have dimensions large enough to allow this operation. The most suitable cavity to hold the bonsai is established and it is filled with a light layer of potting soil which will form the basis for the roots. The bonsai is placed in the cavity, after cleaning the roots and having them covered with soil and peat. Anchor the tree with wire, as described in Ishitsuki on the rock, making sure that the wire keeps the roots well adhered to the soil of the cables and that the tree is as firm as possible. If necessary, it is good to anchor in several places. Also, in this case, the soil is constantly kept humid and care will be taken that the bonsai is not exposed too directly to the sun or wind.

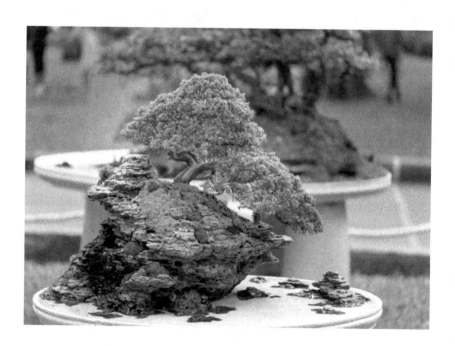

SAIKEI AND BONKEI

These two art forms are related to the nearby bonsai, as they are for creating particular landscapes. Saikei in fact is the art of composing a landscape, combining bonsai with small statuettes, houses and buildings of various types.

To compose a similar aspect, you need an idea of a particular and imaginative scenography on which trees and other elements are displayed, giving the impression of observing a portion of nature in miniature. It is also necessary to carefully take care of the proportions between the various components, as well as the colors and the perspective. To dare a more natural and wild aspect it is better than the trees are of different ages and sizes, as for every group bonsai.

Bonkei is used in rock Saikei. This composition is of particular importance for the Zen tradition, in fact, it implies an attempt to grasp the deep essence of the rock.

All the difficulty, therefore, lies in enhancing the reading of the composition through the arrangement of the elements, the colors, the shapes, up to obtaining a landscape that knows how to show calm and tranquility but also robustness and vital energy

1)Hokidachi; 2) Fukinagashi; 3) Bunjingi; 4)Ishit-
suki on the rock; 5) Ishitsuki in the rock

CHAPTER 4

Bonsai Care

We are now going to take a closer look at the actual work that characterizes bonsai art, starting from the fundamental part that concerns pruning up to the simplest, but no less important, operations of watering and fertilization.

First of all, it is good to know that bonsai needs daily care and needs, like all plants, to maintain particular rhythms and habits.

The ability of a bonsai artist also lies in being able to respect the woods of his plant. However, there are some rules that it is good to follow to get a good bonsai, and that concern each of the five parts of which a plant is made, starting from the roots to get to the top.

Let's see them in detail:

- **Roots**: It is important that the roots develop in all directions so as to allow a better grip on the ground and more adequate nourishment.

- **Trunk:** The trunks must have a solid and robust base and progressively thin upwards. The older the trunk appears, worn from years and from natural damage, such as cracks in the bark, lightning strikes, the more the bonsai acquires value.

- **Branches**: The branches must have a fixed arrangement, the larger ones must extend to the sides, while the smaller ones upwards. The branches that grow on the front, those that start from the same point of the trunk, and those that develop horizontally in a regular way are not very appreciated.

- **Leaves:** The leaves must always be proportionate to the rest of the bonsai. They must remain small and cover the branches creating a thick crown.

- **Top:** The top in the bonsai tradition symbolizes life, it must, therefore, be vital and robust. A broken or ruined top is never considered valuable, except when it gives the tree a desired air of austerity.

PRUNING

One of the beautiful aspects of doing Bonsai is that it's not about working on something static but on something alive and continuously malleable.

I have always thought about painters: working for a long time on a painting; their hands expertly transform a blank canvas into something that can arouse very strong sensations. I believe that the culminating moment for a painter is the last brushstroke, when an idea, his idea, takes shape, when the painting is finished. The picture is finished. And there will no longer be the moments when that idea belonged to him, when it was inside him and pushed him to desire the painting itself.

Afterward, many compliments will be made, the painting will be admired by many people, but the most important thing, the inspiration that the painter dared at that moment, the immense happiness that was procured to him by that last brushstroke, isn't there anymore. Now his idea no longer belongs to him, it is shared with others.

And the only way not to get lost is to start over, start a new painting. I could be wrong, but I think it's very sad.

We, and by us I mean those who grow Bonsai, are luckier: our painting, if we know how to take care of it, will never end, it will change continuously. The bad thing consists in the eventual death of the plant; at least a painter, afterward, can look at his picture.

This is precisely the pruning: the removal, not inconsiderate, of the young vegetation, aimed at the conservation and beautification of the form of the plant. If we don't do that, we will soon find ourselves having a plant that is not exactly a «Bonsai».

And therefore it is one of the most important ways to make your bonsai grow in the way that you want it to is to prune it on a semi-regular basis.

Pruning, in fact, is the main job that allows us to keep a small tree, as it gives us the opportunity to modify and control the natural plant development.

By cutting a branch, in fact, it is prevented from continuing to grow and forces them to develop small sub-branches that will form a 10 crown. However, it is good to consider that there are different ways of pruning depending on the style and the type of tree you want to grow.

There are two different types of pruning techniques that are needed: maintenance pruning, which refines and maintains the structure of the bonsai; and structural pruning, which is more aggressive but gives the bonsai a more basic or natural style.

Before knowing the difference between these two techniques, it is important to fully understand how trees grow and act within their natural environment. Understanding how trees grow and why they respond to certain conditions will help you prune them effectively.

Trees, naturally, have a tendency toward apical dominance, which means their trunks will almost always grow bigger and stronger than their side stems and other offshoots. And this dominance carries on throughout the entire tree. The main trunk has smaller branches, but those smaller branches will be dominant over other smaller branches. This sequence carries on until only the foliage is left.

This is a natural mechanism that many trees have to grow taller instead of casting shade over other trees next to them. But this apical dominance also causes the tree to keep distributing growth to the top and outer branches and this ultimately causes the inner branches to die. This is normal in nature, but it can be aesthetically unpleasing to the eye in the world of growing bonsais.

Once an enthusiast knows the natural growth patterns of a tree, they are able to use pruning techniques to counter the negative aesthetic effects of apical dominance. Since dominant growth occurs in a tree's trunk, it's easy to surmise that the top and outer portions of the bonsai should be pruned more thoroughly. This pruning forces the tree to redistribute growth to the inner and lower parts of the tree, which gives the enthusiast control over the growth of the tree, the thickness of the trunk, and the overall aesthetics of the bonsai.

STRUCTURAL PRUNING

If you have grown your bonsai from a seed/seedling and you have waited for a few years for it to get to the place where you can start pruning it, there will come a time where the tree is strong enough to be pruned and shaped according to what you would like. Structural pruning involves removing larger branches from your bonsai and shaping it into the tree that you want it to be. But, this is a rather stressful process for most enthusiasts because even though the large branches will grow back, the first structural pruning will determine the growth pattern and the overall look of the bonsai. Therefore, it's necessary to carefully consider what type of style you would like for your bonsai. Do take into consideration what species of tree you are growing and what styles suit it. Once you have considered the style and decided on the right one, carefully consider which branches would need to be pruned to start the process of the style.

Because these prunings are rather traumatic on the bonsai, it's better to rather perform them in early spring or late autumn. This enables the bonsai to either enter or exit a growing season. Both of these are normally successful, but if your species of bonsai doesn't cope well in cold weather, it will be better not to prune it in late autumn because the tree will have the combination of cold weather and the trauma of pruning which may kill it.

To start this type of pruning, place your bonsai on a table and look at it from eye level. Start by removing all of the dead foliage and branches from the tree. Once that is completed, start analyzing the bonsai and decide which larger branches you want to remove. This includes all of the branches that block the view of the main trunk, branches that cross over with each other, and disproportionately thick branches at the top of the bonsai.

It is an unfortunate fact that pruning thick branches will leave scarring on the bonsai but this can be reduced if you use concave bonsai cutters. Since your bonsai is an aesthetic work of art, it is worth investing in these types of cutters to reduce the effects of scarring and keep the bonsai as pristine as possible.

If your bonsai is healthy, you can safely remove up to 1/3 of its foliage (which is the same percentage of roots you are allowed to prune before putting your bonsai in danger), but this type of "big" maintenance should only be performed once a year. Anything more can, and most likely will, damage your tree and cause it to die prematurely.

Before embarking on the pruning operation, you must have a clear understanding of the shape you want to give the plant so that you know where to start. We take the appropriate tools, such as simple bonsai and bud shears, and get to work, remembering some basic rules, which are indispensable for obtaining the necessary effects of harmony and balance.

First of all, the branches must not grow in the lower part of the trunk. Usually, the branches are started to develop at a third of the total length of the trunk, to give the plant greater impetus.

It is important to take into great consideration the point where the plant is observed; in this way, it will be evident, as we have seen, that the branches that grow on the front of the plant are useless, while those on the sides and on the back will be accentuated.

To give a livelier image to the bonsai, while maintaining a harmonious appearance, it is good to avoid the branches that grow at the same height and parallel, and also, during pruning, remember not to prune all the branches to the same size, but to leave different lengths.

If you want to limit the growth of a branch, to keep it small, it is sufficient to trim it, otherwise, it will develop and strengthen.

It is advisable to carry out pruning in the period of the year in which the crown is developed, so as to have undergone a clear image of the cuts that are being practiced on the bonsai.

Finally, it is very important, when you want to cut a whole branch, as close as possible to the trunk, by leveling the cut, so as to hide the wound from sight. For this purpose, the use of concave shears is recommended. In addition, in the case of particularly deep wounds, it is good to use a suitable disinfectant to be purchased from a nurseryman. Sometimes to give an older image to the bonsai, a special tool is used, called a jinning forceps.

This allows the branches to be cut so as to leave part of the bark of the branch attached to the trunk, giving the impression that the tree has been affected by lightning.

For use of pruning to direct the growth of branches. By pruning the branch, a just above a bud facing downwards we will obtain a branch that will grow upwards after drawing a curve.

The dashes in the two sequences, show the branches that are of no use for the formation of any bonsai style, therefore they must be pruned

How to trim the shoots of a conifer

This technique is particularly difficult and still requires some experience in order not to ruin the plant.

Finally, it's advisable to do some shopping online and purchase a cut-paste that you can apply to all of the wounds on the bonsai after pruning. Infections in trees aren't uncommon and if you have spent a lot of time and effort on your bonsai, the last thing you want to do is lose it because of a bad cut. Bonsai cut-pastes prevent infections and promote faster healing.

MAINTENANCE PRUNING

The primary goal of maintenance pruning is to prevent a bonsai from acting as it would in nature. Once a tree starts to focus its growth towards the top and outer branches, the bonsai doesn't really look pleasing to the eye any longer. So, maintenance pruning needs to be employed on a regular basis to keep it from growing in areas where it isn't supposed to. When those areas are pruned away, the tree naturally sends the nutrients to the trunk and starts to increase in size centrally — this results in a much better-looking bonsai.

If you are unsure when to prune your bonsai, it depends on whether you keep your bonsai outdoors or indoors. Outdoor bonsais should only be pruned during the growing seasons of spring and summer. Since the cold makes the tree go dormant and doesn't send a lot of nutrients to the foliage, it's redundant to prune during the cold months. But, if you have an indoor bonsai, you can prune all-year-round because the bonsai will remain warmer inside and, thus, not have a dormant period.

Unlike pruning rose bushes, you don't need to excessively prune your bonsai when you're maintaining its shape. Only prune the areas that start growing too quickly. If a branch becomes too long or the canopy is uneven, then snip those parts off.

Use sharp scissors to skip away at the branches and maintain the leaves, but if you have a pine or another coniferous bonsai, it's better to rather pinch the branches off with your fingers because snipping it with scissors can lead to unsightly brown discolorations and dead foliage at the pruning sites. Since the bonsai is still small, the branches are tender enough to easily be pinched off by hand.

Some bonsais are better pruned with scissors, while others are better pruned with your fingers, but some actually need a combination of the two depending on the type of tree and strength of the branches. Hence, adequate research on your bonsai is necessary to know exactly what is the best method of maintenance pruning.

CUTTING LEAVES AND BUDS

It happens that an indoor bonsai throws the buds all year round, so pruning leaves and buds are an almost daily practice.

However, it is easy to apply, in fact, the rules to follow are less numerous than for pruning branches. The important thing is to remember that where a sprout is left there, a branch will develop, while the lower part of the trunk will be strengthened and the branching will become thinner. In any case, it is good to remember that the leaves must always be cut leaving a piece of a stalk and that the direction of the last leaf a stalk left after cutting also determines the direction of the bud that will grow later.

It is recommended to always cut the biggest leaves. As for the plants that bloom, pruning will only be done after the development of the flowers.

While for subtropical plants the right period for cutting shoots and leaves is between spring and autumn, tropical plants, which grow all year round, will always be pruned and pruned.

In conifers, the topping of the shoots, an operation sometimes performed simply with the nails, will cause many small needles to develop. In short, the cutting of the leaves allows us to obtain three main results: A thin branching, the shrinking of the leaves and greater ventilation of the crown of the branches.

Every year, in the period between March and August, it is good to proceed with the total defoliation of the tree; in doing so, the plant is stimulated to develop new shoots in a short time, accelerating vegetative growth. Smaller leaves and thinner branches will grow under the petioles, giving the bonsai the classic appearance of a dwarf tree.

*Effects of
leaf pruning*

APPLICATION OF THE METAL WIRE

We now pass to another very important moment, that of the application of the metal wire, which is essential for the tree to grow according to the desired shape.

Pruning is a very important part of shaping your bonsai, but if you want to truly shape your bonsai into the shape you desire, then you will need to take it a step further and wire your bonsai.

To obtain well-defined shapes, without which the Bonsai would not be so real, that is, wouldn't resemble a life-sized tree, binding is necessary. And so, by lowering a branch or bending the trunk, we can create an exceptionally natural effect in its artificiality and enchant the observer, placing him in front of a tree a few centimeters high but which he has already seen, at another time, in another place, probably in a wood and several meters high. This is the magic of Bonsai.

By wrapping wire around the trunk and branches of your bonsai, you are able to manipulate exactly where and how you want the branches to grow. When the tree is flexible, it's easy to move the bonsai into the position that you would like, but it's rather complicated to keep it there. Having the sturdiness of the wire allows for the tree to be molded and then remain in the position it was placed in. It will take a few months, but as soon as the branches are set, the wire can be removed. The bonsai will continue to grow in the style that it was adjusted into.

Bonsais can be wired at any time of year and it can be performed at your own preference. The only species of trees that should be wired in winter are deciduous trees and any other trees that lose their leaves in colder temperatures. The reason for this is because it's much easier to wire the bonsais when your vision isn't obstructed by foliage. But it is important to pay attention during this time because even though the nutrients in foliage don't go to the foliage, large branches can grow thicker in the winter months and, if this occurs, it can create scarring if the wires start digging into the flesh of the branches.

If you notice that the branches are growing at an accelerated rate, remove the wiring around the bonsai and replace it at a later stage. Scarring from wires that have broken the bark of a bonsai will most likely be permanent, so it should be avoided as best as possible.

TYPES OF WIRES

There are two types of wires that can be considered when wiring bonsais:

Suitable wires are copper or aluminum and for some types of trees, such as maple, apricot and thorns, it is convenient to use plastic-coated threads or wrapped in paper. They are metallic threads, very soft to fold and shape, suitable for being rolled around the wood we want to put into shape. But it is also difficult to straighten, especially when it stays on the tree for some time exposed to atmospheric agents. A branch left wrapped in aluminum wire for a few months takes the desired shape and maintains it even after the wire is removed.

Neither one of these wires rust and both have a strong tensile strength. Aluminum wire is better for use in deciduous bonsais, while copper wire is better for use in pine and conifer trees. That being said, the aluminum wire does work well with practically all species of bonsais and is the easiest to use as a beginner enthusiast.

The diameter will be of different sizes depending on the thickness and strength of the branch to be corrected. Usually, a wire 1/3 of the diameter of the branch or trunk to be wrapped is used. Wires come in a variety of thicknesses (1 - 8 mm) but the best ones for beginners don't exceed 4 mm in thickness. The thicker wires should be used on the larger branches and you can use thinner wires as you move up and along the bonsai. It is best to first wrap the trunk and thick branches in palm fiber (raffia) that has been soaked in water. This prevents scarring on the thicker sections of the bonsai. If thinner branches are scarred, they can always be removed, but this isn't a possibility with the trunk and main branches. So extra precautions are necessary.

HOW TO WIRE YOUR BONSAI

Wiring your bonsai is going to be very tricky and you are going to make mistakes. But as you have learned to be more patient with the entire growing process of your bonsai, you will get the technique right when you practice it. While you are still starting out, consider double-wiring certain branches that are close together because wrapping them together allows support for the branches and allows slightly more space for you to work.

Before proceeding with the application, it is advisable to fix the wire to the ground or to the trunk, always starting from the backside, so as to hide the origin of the binding or not to leave too much play.

Especially for the first case, in fact, it would damage the bark of the tree, risking the wire embedding itself in the bonsai. In this case, it is better to cut the metal wire and leave the part embedded in the shaft, to avoid even greater injuries. The wire should be wound at an angle of 45 degrees to the trunk or branch, avoiding tying both leaves and buds.

The period of time in which to maintain the binding is different depending on the style chosen and the type of tree: Indicatively, it varies from 6-8 months of deciduous plants to 18 months of conifers. The thread will preferably be removed in the autumn before the vegetative stasis. It is good to remember not to apply during the vegetative awakening of the plant, not to practice it on newly repotted or repotted bonsai trees, as each of these operations considerably weakens the plant.

Once the wire has been applied, the plant will be kept in a place sheltered from the sun and wind, spraying and watering often. Unfortunately, the aluminum wire cannot be left permanently on the tree. In fact, all trees, especially in autumn, swell the trunk and branches.

This happens, to a proportionately reduced extent, even in Bonsai. Therefore, when the wire becomes too tight, the wood begins to come out of the spaces between one coil and the other, until it completely covers the wire and incorporates it (not immediately but within a few years). At this point there is nothing more to do: if we remove the wire, we will irreparably damage the bark of the Bonsai, causing a large leak of lymph with consequent death of the plant; while if we leave it, in the long run, it will suffocate the plant.

Every month look closely at the plant in the points where it is wrapped with the thread and when you realize that the thread has become too tight, remove it. It is easy to notice when the wire begins to tighten as the part of the wire in contact with the bark enters it slightly and the wood adheres perfectly to the wire and begins to incorporate it. Once the thread has been removed, you will notice that the bark is slightly marked by the imprints of the threads: do not worry, the marks will disappear within a year.

The cutter is used to remove the aluminum wire. It has very long handles, to be able to penetrate between the branches without breaking them and the particular shape of the blades allows it to cut the wire perfectly without cutting the bark. Alternatively, the only way is to do it with your hands, or rather with your fingers.

Never cut the wire with an electrician's wire cutters or scissors, since due to the shape of the blades, it is practically impossible not to damage the bark. Here's how to proceed with unwinding the thread by hand: gently but with a steady hand, take the branch wrapped in the thread between thumb and forefinger and with the other hand, still holding it between thumb and forefinger, lift the terminal tip of the thread. Now, without twisting the branch, unwind the thread in the opposite way to the direction of the coils until it is completely removed from the tree.

Pay close attention to where the branch attaches to the trunk because this is where you could cause a break. Never proceed in the opposite direction of what was explained above.

If by chance the wire is too large in diameter and you are unable to grab the tip to unwind it, get yourself a pair of small pliers and carefully lift the end of the wire. A tip: if you decide to remove the thread, don't do that immediately but first let the earth dry in the pot, avoiding watering the plant for a couple of days (if it is not summer, because in this period the earth dries up within a few hours): in this way, there will be less lymph circulation in the plant and the branches will be much more elastic, therefore there will be less chances of breaking the wood.

The metal wire is the main technique for changing the shape of the plant; however, there are other ways to correct it.

Once you have got the hang of this method, use single-wiring on the branches that can't be double-wired. Don't shape the branches until you have wrapped the entire tree because if you start shaping it too early you may get confused with what to do with the remainder of the branches if you designed your desired style. Waiting until the end to shape allows you to move everything more smoothly and sequentially.

When wiring an entire bonsai, start at the bottom of the trunk and then move up to the primary branches. Once those are done, use a thinner wire to wrap the secondary branches and up into the foliage. As a general rule, use a wire that is 1/3 as thick as the branch that you are wiring. That thickness will allow for enough structural support to style the bonsai.

After you have completed the entire process of wiring the bonsai (which will take a long time, so be patient), you can start to form it into the shape you desire. Grip the branches firmly with your thumb and index finger and start bending them slowly. Even though the branches are flexible, they can still break, so move slowly and gently. Once the branch is positioned, do not move it again.

Once your bonsai has been styled according to your specifications, move it outside and into a shady spot if it's in the warmer months. Fertilize your bonsai as you normally would and keep a close eye on it because you don't want the tree to grow and get scarred. When you remove the wiring, you need to cut the wires at every turn and not unwind it. Unwinding the wiring almost always damages the bark on the bonsai and it will leave avoidable scarring.

In fact, you can also use cords attached to the container, to another support, or to the trunk itself to keep the branches in tension. Other times stones or weights can be tied to a branch in order to change its direction of development.

Finally, with small wooden dowels, it is possible to spread two branches considered too close.

Of all these techniques, however, that of the metal wire is the most used, as it allows a more precise action on the branches and on the trunk.

WATERING AND FERTILIZING

There are several fundamentals of growing bonsais but two of the most integral are watering and fertilizing sufficiently. These factors are all dependent on the species of the bonsai, the size of the tree, the season, the size of the container, and how much sunlight the bonsai receives. It is necessary to research exactly how much water and fertilizer your bonsai needs, but there are a few basic guidelines that you can follow to ensure that your bonsai remains healthy.

SUCCESSFUL WATERING

If one of the most frequent causes of death of a plant is the incorrect location of the plant itself, the absolute greatest cause is certainly watering. Everything is said about the amount of water that a Bonsai needs, even if it is by far one of the simplest things to do correctly.

There are those who are afraid of too much watering and water them just once a week (since Bonsai are indoor plants), there are those who are afraid of too little watering and put the pot in hydroculture, and there are those who say they give only a few drops of water so as not to make the Bonsai grow.

The first rule of successful watering is not to water your tree while the soil is still wet, but it's also important not to let the soil get dry either. There needs to be a careful balance between the two because overly wet soil can cause root rot and too dry soil can cause the roots to become brittle which will cause them to die. While you are still learning how to judge this process, place your finger about ½ an inch into the soil and feel for the moisture content. If you think that it's becoming slightly dry, then you should water your tree. The longer you perform this, the more experience you will gain and the more you will be able to judge by sight when your bonsai needs to be watered.

The second rule is never to water on a routine. If you have multiple bonsai, you may be tempted to water on a routine, but this can be detrimental to your trees because you may be overwatering some and underwatering others. Judge each bonsai individually and ensure that they all receive water when they need it.

The final rule is to water gently. Water that's being poured out rapidly can move the soil too rapidly and damage some of the roots. It's imperative to use a watering can that has a fine nozzle to disperse the water evenly over the top of the soil without displacing it. This type of nozzle will also keep you from overwatering your bonsais.

Watering, so it is another very important phase in the care of a bonsai. It must be practiced often with extreme care, so as not to damage the plant. The bonsai, in fact, because of its restricted root system, it does not draw sustenance from the soil for a long time.

It is therefore necessary to keep it supplied with moist soil rich in nutrients. It is a good rule to water the soil only when it is dry or slightly damp; watering when the soil is still wet can cause more damage than advantages.

Some tricks allow us, however, to easily understand if it is really necessary to water. The first concerns the color that the soil takes on: it will be drier the more the color becomes clear.

A dark color instead indicates that the earth is still steeped in water.

The need for water from the bonsai can also be ascertained by simply knocking against the container and listening to the sound produced. Usually, an empty sound shows that the earth has dried up, detaching itself from the edges of the vase; on the contrary, a full muffled sound will indicate that the earth is dilated by water and adheres well to the container.

Types of water

There are 3 types of water that we can use to water our bonsai.

• **Tap water:** it will certainly be the best choice. Given the presence of chlorosis, it is advisable to fill a small container with water and use it the next day so that the chlorine evaporates. For very hard water rich in limestone, it is advisable to put 1 cm of white peat in the bottom of the water collection container, which thanks to its acidity partially dampens the effect of limestone dissolved in the water. It may seem like an unnecessary refinement, but you may find, after some time, the earth of the bonsai very hard: it has made the so-called "brick effect" and could stress the plant. Surely this problem does not exist in high mountain areas where water has a very low hardness.

• **Well water:** it is certainly the best as it is rich in mineral salts, at the right temperature and, as a rule, with a relatively low level of hardness.

• **Rainwater:** it is still collected, even if, especially that of the first rains, is acidic. Unfortunately, it is thought that problems such as acid rain do not affect us, but it is not always the case: if acidic water can create problems to a potted plant that is cared for and pampered, let's imagine what devastating phenomena it could cause to wood.

If by chance the rains are excessively acidic in the area where you live, you can throw limestone rocks or sodium bicarbonate into the water collection tank to correct the pH of the water; but at these levels, it is better to fall back on other types of water.

Let's forget about distilled water because it is totally devoid of mineral salts which are instead used by the plant, and which are contained in all the other types of water we have seen. If possible, also purified tap water should be avoided as it could be harmful to the plant.

Warning: never water with hot or lukewarm water, the water must be cold, or rather, at room temperature.

It is usually watered when the earth in the pot is dry.

With the tip of your finger, gently move the first soil in the pot to reveal the one below and if you feel that it is still wet it means that the plant does not need water.

Beware of days when there is a lot of wind: the wind dries the earth in the pots impressively.

However, the most recurring question is the one concerning the quantity of water to be given to a plant; at the end of this chapter, you will find a table that collects most of the plants available as bonsai and their proper watering. A general rule: if you want to know how much water a plant needs, look at how it is in nature. An elm, amidst rains and veins of water underground, is used to receiving an abundant quantity of water. A pomegranate, native to very dry and hot climates, lives very well, even in summer, with little water.

In spring, summer and autumn, it is very important to respect certain watering times.

Plants must be watered early in the morning or in the evening after sunset. Watering them when it is very hot, pouring cold water into the earth which is probably hot, causes a serious shock to the plant. So remember: water in the morning until 8 am or in the evening after 8 pm. In winter, of course, we can water when we prefer, however never in the evening, as ice could form on the roots during the night. In spring and summer water once a day.

Two methods are mainly used for watering: Either the water is poured onto the soil surface through a watering can, or the container is directly immersed in the water. In the first case, it will be necessary to proceed slowly, to allow time for the soil to fully impregnate.

When the water comes out of the drain hole, the soil will have been properly watered. In the event, however, that the water cannot penetrate the soil, but escapes from the edge of the container, it means that the earth is too dry and we will proceed in the other way.

The second method is equally simple. The containers are immersed in water to bring bubbles of air to the surface. When no more bubbles come out, the soil will be completely drenched with water and the bonsai can be rearranged in its place.

The bonsai however change their water needs in the changing seasons. In summer it will be necessary to water more frequently, at least twice a day, making sure that the soil does not dry out too much. However, we recommend watering early in the morning and in the evening with water at room temperature.

Furthermore, especially in the city, it is important to spray the leaves during the day to eliminate the smog and dust layer that can be created. However, you have to remember not to do it in the evening, because the plant could get sick or be damaged in any case.

Furthermore, during the summer period, miniature and rock bonsai trees need more water than normal bonsai, as well as deciduous trees since the rather large surface of the leaves increases transudation.

In the autumn season, however, the need for water decreases, the leaves fall, and the plant prepares for winter stasis. In any case, it will be good to frequently check the humidity conditions in order not to experience unpleasant inconveniences.

With winter, the phase of least demand for water is reached, as the tree slows down most of its functions and enters a period of substantial inactivity.

It is therefore sufficient to water 2-3 times a week, preferably during the afternoon hours to avoid night frost.

Only conifers maintain their need for water rather high since the foliar apparatus does not fall during the autumn and needs continuous nourishment.

With spring, however, the full activity of the tree begins again, the shoots reappear and the demand for water resumes, which will increase more and more over time, as we get closer to summer.

SUCCESSFUL FERTILIZING

Another widespread belief is that Bonsai remain small only if they are not fertilized. I deny it for the umpteenth time. To make it grow healthy, you've got to make sure you feed the plant providing it with the needed substances.

Depending on the period, certain substances, which are different and serve different purposes, must be supplied to the Bonsai. If the needs of the tree are respected, we will be able to enjoy splendid moments, not only the spring budding, but also flowering and fruiting; sights that manage, with their delicacy, to melt even the hardest hearts.

Fertilization is extremely simple and with the following indications, you can't go wrong. Among other things, even in the case of a higher fertilizer dose, serious issues will not occur.

Any gardener knows that fertilizing their plants from time to time will ensure their health and make them far more vibrant, and this is a mentality that all bonsai enthusiasts need to adopt too. Because fertilizing your bonsai regularly during the growing season is paramount for the tree to not only survive but to thrive.

Types of fertilizers:

There are numerous elements dissolved in the soil that are absorbed by the plant from the roots, but the three elements that interest us are nitrogen, potassium and phosphorus. The first, nitrogen, is used to make vegetation grow: everything that is green in a plant is facilitated in its development by nitrogen. Potassium and phosphorus are used by the plant to develop wood, flowers and fruits. Many of you, at this point, will be frightened, thinking how difficult must be to obtain these elements. Don't worry, nitrogen is found in dry cow manure and phosphorus and potassium in chicken manure.

There is no need (fortunately) to obtain them at home, even if, perhaps, you have both a cow and a hen available; these elements, ready for use, are easily found in any flower shop, just ask for nitrogen fertilizer and a potassium-based one.

As with all plants, bonsais require a fertilizer that's well-balanced in nitrogen, potassium, and phosphorus. There are times that you can change the concentrations, but that is normally reserved for expert-level enthusiasts. As a beginner enthusiast, it is encouraged just to use fertilizers that are equal in all three amounts with other micronutrients included.

During the growth period, fertilization must be carried out every twenty days, going as far as fertilizing also every week, during the autumn, to prepare the plant for the winter period. In winter, fertilization is superfluous for many bonsai as the plant stops its vegetative development.

On each package of any type of fertilizer, you will find an abbreviation, for example: n.p.k. 6.19.19. This abbreviation indicates the percentages of substances that the real powder or liquid taken into consideration can provide to the plant once placed in the soil. The abbreviation mentioned above means: nitrogen 6%, phosphorus 19%, potassium 19%. That is a fertilizer poor in nitrogen but rich in potassium and phosphorus. On the contrary, a fertilizer signed n.p.k. 18.7.7 will be high in nitrogen and low in phosphorus/potassium. It will be convenient to have both types at home, and by this, I do not intend to have two fertilizers with the percentages I have mentioned but to buy one rich in nitrogen and one rich in phosphorus and potassium.

Avoid choosing fertilizers with very high percentages (let's say over 20%) because they could have too strong effects on the bonsai: remember that yours must live in a small pot. You should not use too powerful fertilizers such as guano, which, if for certain uses is more than excellent, has a truly devastating effect on bonsai.

Only conifers are to be fertilized as early as January as they resume activity before other plants. Fertilization should always be carried out after the flowering period, to prevent the flowering branches from absorbing too much nourishment and losing the flowers. Remember also that it is good not to start immediately after repotting or pruning the roots, as the injured parts would be damaged.

It's necessary to follow the specifications on the fertilizer you purchase. Some fertilizers are more concentrated than others and overfeeding your bonsai is a possibility. But bonsai fertilizers normally come in cubes and can be included directly on the ground around the bonsai itself. However, these fertilizer cubes can be picked up by birds if you have your bonsai outside so you will need to protect them. It's best to cover them with cups or baskets that allow water to pass through easily. Water as you normally would until the fertilizer cubes are dissolved.

Alternatively, bonsai fertilizer can also be purchased in liquid form. This can be diluted directly into your watering can and gradually given to your bonsais. Both of these fertilizers are effective and you can use whichever you prefer.

Remember that because the amount of soil in a bonsai pot is limited, there is a limited amount of nutrients available for the tree to use. This means that your bonsai will need extra nutrients from fertilizers. But keep in mind that overfeeding your tree can kill it too, so carefully balance the feeding regime with the guidelines on the fertilizer you purchase.

Fertilizers, furthermore if used correctly, are indispensable to help the development of our bonsai, by integrating and completing the nutrients of the soil.

Deprived of fertilizers the bonsai would live for about a year, therefore it would begin to perish, the leaves would wither and branches and trunk would weaken. This is because the bonsai, being forced into a pot of such a small size after a certain period exhausts the mineral elements necessary for its nourishment. It is therefore important to remember that every bonsai needs a certain amount of nitrogen, phosphorus, potassium, calcium, sulfur, iron and, in smaller quantities, other minerals. We will, therefore, have to look for fertilizers that contain these substances.

Various types of fertilizers are available on the market: Powder, liquids and balls, the latter used mainly for outdoor bonsai but also very suitable for indoor bonsai.

Furthermore, a distinction is also made between organic fertilizers, namely those derived from organic fabrics, such as bone meal, blood-based fertilizers, etc., and inorganic fertilizers, such as salt compounds.

For good fertilization, it is however essential to follow some rules.

First of all, the fertilizer should be administered especially during the growing season of the plant, helping it with all the necessary nourishment; it is, the youngest bonsai to need more help, precisely for their very rapid growth.

Once you have chosen the most suitable period and the type of fertilizer you can move on to the practical phase.

Water abundantly and prepare the dose of fertilizer as indicated on the package; in fact, the dose for a bonsai does not differ much from that normally recommended.

This is how we proceed to fertilization, remembering these tips:

-       It is always better to fertilize little, but often, rather than a lot and rarely because in this way the food is distributed more regularly over time, without risking excesses.

-       Liquid fertilizers are absorbed faster, so it will be necessary to fertilize more often. On the contrary, powder fertilizers dissolve more slowly in the soil, allowing a lasting effect.

If the roots get sick, it is good to stop fertilizing until the root system is completely restored

The following indications give the precise fertilizing times, suitable for all plants, and are to be considered the annual fertilization calendar:

January: Do not fertilize.

February: Do not fertilize.

March: Do not fertilize.

April: Half a dose of nitrogen in the middle of the month.

May: 1 nitrogen dose in the middle of the month.

June: 1 dose of nitrogen in the middle of the month.

July: Do not fertilize.

August: Do not fertilize.

September: Half dose of nitrogen at the beginning of the month; 1 dose of phosphorus/potassium in the second half of the month.

October: 1 dose of phosphorus/potassium in the middle of the month.

November: Do not fertilize.

December: Do not fertilize.

CHAPTER 5

Plant Diseas

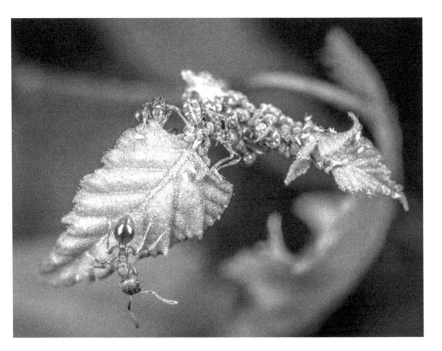

We now begin a very important chapter in the care of bonsai, as it can often happen that a plant shows symptoms of a disease that is difficult to recognize and, therefore, to cure. In fact, due to its size, the bonsai is more defenseless than the normal plants against the attacks of many adversities, therefore it is the bonsai artist's job to quickly recognize the diseases and help his plant.

Bonsai are attacked by numerous natural enemies, such as insects and, unfortunately, even fungi. Furthermore, serious problems can occur due to incorrect watering or too much sun; problems, which, if taken in time, are quite simple to solve but, if neglected, can lead to the death of the plant.

When the bonsai begins to weaken, it is immediately necessary to check whether there are deficiencies or excesses of some kind in its care and maintenance: In what position is the plant about to the wind and light? At what level are humidity and temperature? Is it fed in the right way? All these factors must always be kept under control, but sometimes the bad health of our bonsai can derive from other causes.

Bonsai trees, like most other plants on earth, are susceptible to parasites, fungi, and insects that can greatly damage them. Since there are so many things that can attack your bonsai, the best case of treatment, in this case, is prevention. If you keep your tree healthy, it will be able to fight off many infections and fungi without much external help, because many trees can mount their own defenses against these attacks.

If you balance your water, fertilizer, and light requirements for your bonsai, it will most likely stay healthy and continue to grow for years. But one of the worst problems that enthusiasts make is to put their bonsai in the wrong location. If the tree doesn't have good lighting and good air circulation, it will be more susceptible to developing a problem.

Additionally, it is necessary that you keep the area around your bonsai as hygienic as possible. If you take the effort of cleaning the area where your bonsais are situated, there is a greatly reduced risk of your tree(s) developing problems, but sometimes there are problems that can arise that even healthy trees can't ward off — pests.

ANIMAL AND PLANT PESTS

It is important to bear in mind that bonsai are subject to the same pests and diseases as the species of the trees to which they belong. Therefore, in principle, as regards diseases due to plant or animal parasites, a bonsai, if in full force, has the potential to defend itself. A constant cure would, therefore, be sufficient to prevent and avoid diseases of this type. However, this does not exclude that, during the weakening phases due to repotting or pruning, the bonsai can get sick. Among the animal parasites, we find various types of insects that damage the plant by using it for their nourishment.

The most common are:

* *Ants*

Description: Ants on your bonsai are a dangerous sign because ants and aphids normally work together. The reason for this is because ants and aphids have a co-dependent relationship where the ants carry the eggs of aphids to suitable vegetation because the aphids will eventually produce a sweet, sugary substance known as "honeydew" which the ants thrive on. The ants aren't really a problem on your bonsai, but their little passengers are definitely something to worry about.

Ants may not be a problem themselves, but the problems that they carry with them can be severely devastating to your bonsai. Ants don't only carry aphid eggs, but they can also carry a black sooty fungus that starts to destroy the bark of trees. Additionally, ants are known to make their nests in bonsai pots and can disrupt the root system of your bonsai.

Symptoms: If you notice that ants are starting to nest in your bonsai's pot, then it indicates that you aren't watering your tree correctly. But, in the cases of trees like pines, which prefer drier soil, sometimes this can't be changed because adding additional water could hurt your tree.

Cure: In cases like these, it's better to use a gentle pesticide that won't hurt the roots of your tree. Pesticides like Bungy, Kemprin, and Koinor are your best options for treating problems at a root level.

- *Anthracnose*

Description: Anthracnose is an umbrella term that includes several fungal infections that affect trees. These fungi thrive on plant material where it inoculates and then spreads very quickly. If a bonsai is kept in a warm, humid, shady place, these fungi will spread like wildfire and damage your bonsai.

Unfortunately, during the warmth of the growing seasons along with young foliage starting to develop, anthracnose is a serious risk and you need to keep a close eye on any signs of it developing. When leaves become thicker and more leathery, they are far more resilient to fungal infections, but young leaves are very susceptible.

Symptoms: The symptoms of these types of infections are very easy to spot, but they still seem to go unnoticed by enthusiasts who don't know what they're looking for. One of the indicative symptoms is the drying and curling of leaves that look like they've been burned. As the fungal infection worsens, more and more brown spots will spread to more leaves and will continuously look like the tree is being scorched even though it may be in a shady spot.

Not all trees are susceptible to these types of infections and they are practically unheard of in species like conifers and evergreens. Deciduous trees, on the other hand, have much softer leaves and seem to be far more susceptible to these types of infections

Even though these types of infections are rather unsightly on your bonsai, they aren't normally severe enough to kill the tree. They usually only cause the death of one or two branches at a time, but if left untreated, it can eventually spread into the trunk of the tree and that can lead to its death.

Cure: If you notice that your bonsai is infected with this type of infection, it will spread to your other trees and plants if you aren't careful. It is important to quarantine any bonsais with these possible infections and keep them away from other plants. Just like human infections, these types of infections can spread very easily to any other plants close to them so quarantining them is one of the best actions.

Once that is done, spray your tree with chemical sprays designed to treat anthracnose infections and repeat the treatment until it starts working. It is also necessary to remove all of the infected leaves and branches as far as possible and spray the rest of the tree down on a daily basis. Keep the tree in a highly lit area and watch the bonsai closely for any brown spots on the uninfected leaves.

Aphids

Description: Even though an infestation of ants is normally indicative of an aphid infestation, aphids are also known to attack plants by themselves. Aphids are one of the most common and one of the most detrimental pests to bonsais. Aphids burrow into the soft areas of plants and start sucking out the sap. But this has a dual problem because the plant is losing a lot of its nutrients and aphids regularly carry diseases that attack plants from the inside.

Any little bugs that appear to be green, black, or gray are most likely aphids and if you spot them, they should be treated quickly. Aphids attack plants and manage to devour large sections of the plants in a very small amount of time, so it's important to check under your bonsai's leaves on a regular basis to keep any problems from arising.

It is a hemipterus, about 1/1.5 mm long, which has the bad habit of sucking the lymph by attaching itself to the lower part of the leaf. It is clear that, in the long run, it can damage the plant which is forced to produce an enormous amount of lymph that it won't be able to use. Among other things, you won't find just one aphid on the plant: the aphids group into families under each leaf to form small clusters and are infesting, that is, if you find them on a plant, it is very easy that the others are attacked. But there is an alarm signal, a quite evident one, that makes you understand the presence of aphids on your plant: milking ants. You must know that aphids suck lymph and emit, as excrement, a sugary substance that these tiny ants are greedy for. The ant goes after the aphid, hits it on the back and collects the sugary substance released. It's incredible. Therefore, if you see small ants pacing back and forth on your tree trunk, for sure there are aphids. But it is not said that the ants are present, so it is necessary to check every week under the leaves of the tree if there are these unwelcome guests (aphids are very visible) and apply the treatment that we will see shortly.

Aphids can attack the plant in the period between May and September, never in autumn and winter.

Symptoms: If you notice that the leaves and branches on your bonsai seem to be weaker than normal, it could be indicative of an aphid attack. Additionally, if you notice that new leaves that are sprouting seem to be curled and unhealthy, then your suspicions may be confirmed. The reason why the new growth comes out looking like that is that the nutrients are so leached out by the aphids that the tree can't adequately support new growth.

Cure: If this is a problem that is affecting your bonsai, then you will need to wash the leaves with a stream of water. But ensure that you don't harm the tree further. Additionally, there are some gentle baby shampoos that can be used. Make a diluted solution and wash the leaves. The aphids can't breathe with the soap covering them and they either leave or die. A few repetitions of this should clear up the infestation.

Logically, there are generic sprays on the market for the disinfestation of insects that attack plants.

There are also specific ones against aphids. I recommend a pyrethrum-based spray or its derivatives (pyrethrins) because it is an element of natural origin and in case of improper use, there is no risk of possible intoxication. When you notice the presence of aphids under the leaves of your plant, spray a small amount of spray over and under the entire canopy of the tree.

Repeat the operation after a week and the problem will be solved. If after a certain time they reappear, behave as above.

It is very likely that aphids, even when dead, remain on the leaf. This is not harmful but ugly to see. They can be removed with a dry cotton swab or by gently rubbing the leaf plate with your finger. Warning: do not use mosquito sprays or similar, even if based on pyrethrins.

The use for which these sprays were designed is completely different and could seriously damage the plant.

You can consider other insecticides or you can move your bonsai to an area that has a high population of ladybugs. Ladybugs are carnivorous little beetles and they devour aphids without harming your bonsai. There are many insects that you want in your garden and ladybugs are definitely one of them!

- *Borer*

Description: Tree borers consist of different species of insects that lay their eggs on or underneath a tree's bark. When the eggs hatch and the larvae start to squirm out, they immediately look for sustenance and they start to burrow deeper into the tree, eating the woody flesh as they move deeper.

As the larvae grow, their appetites will also increase, and because they may be burrowing into the trunk of your bonsai, there may be serious problems that will develop soon after they get deeper into the lumen.

Symptoms: It is possible to miss the adult insects on your bonsai, but you will notice the signs that larvae have started to burrow into your bonsai. There will be signs of holes and even sawdust around the base of the tree.

Cure: This type of infestation is definitely one of the most difficult to treat and if the larvae have made it into the trunk, it might be untreatable. There are pesticides that you can try, but the real problem is that the death of the wood is going to affect your bonsai's aesthetics forever. If you have other bonsai, it might be best to get rid of the infected bonsai to prevent it from spreading to any of your other trees.

It may be a difficult decision, but it may be the most prudent in cases like these.

- *Caterpillars*

Description: Caterpillars are the larvae stage of butterflies and moths and even though most of their damage is caused above ground, they do have voracious appetites.

Symptoms: Caterpillars of all sixes can consume large quantities of leaves in a very small space of time.

Fortunately, it's very easy to see if caterpillars have attacked your bonsai and you will be able to take action quickly.

Cure: The best treatment, in this case, is to actually remove them by hand. This may be time-consuming, and some caterpillars are small and camouflaged, but it is better for your bonsai and the environment if you are able to avoid using pesticides. It is also useful to make a solution of baby shampoo and rub it on the leaves of your bonsai. If there is a form of soap on the leaves, the caterpillars won't want to eat them.

- *Mealybugs*

Description: Mealybugs are white, furry insects that produce a waxy covering to protect themselves from the elements and from larger predators. These types of insects are found underneath leaves and sometimes in the root systems of plants. So, when you are repotting your bonsai, it's always necessary to check the roots for any indications of these little creatures.

Symptoms: Just like aphids, mealybugs burrow in and start sucking the sap of the tree or plant. Leaves will start to droop and look unhealthy. They will move from vibrant green to a more yellow discoloration until the leaf dies. If left untreated, the tree will take strain because of the lack of nutrients so it does need to be addressed quickly.

Cure: Using an acidic solution of lime or lemon juice in these cases helps for the treatment of mealy bugs and the acid can effectively kill them. If this isn't successful you can increase the treatment to a pesticide that is safe to use on trees.

- *Red Spider Mites*

Description: Red spider mites are a tiny pest and even though they are smaller than aphids, they are much faster moving and can kill a plant at an accelerated rate. Once red spider mites settle on a tree, they get to work very quickly.

The main problem with these types of mites is their size. Because they're so small they are very easy to overlook and not notice. Only if one is very close to the leaves can they see the little mites moving and even then, it's when one knows what they're looking for.

Symptoms: The first indication that enthusiasts normally see that there's a problem is that the leaves on their bonsais start to get yellow and brown blotches on the leaves of their bonsai.

Cure: The treatment for these types of mites is normally with a pesticide because they spread so rapidly. It is best to quarantine your bonsai to prevent further spread and then treat as best as you can. If you catch the infection early and treat the mites rapidly, your bonsai should recover to its full health.

- *White Grubs*

Description: Most pests target the top of the trees but grubs, on the other hand, go straight for the root systems of trees and larger plants. This means that the root systems of bonsais are susceptible to the larvae of several different beetles known as grubs. And, unfortunately, there is no way of knowing there is a problem until the problems start to manifest themselves above ground.

Symptoms: Because grubs attack the roots, the tree will seem healthy at first, but it will start to seem more sickly over time. Pay attention to the leaves of your bonsai and if you notice that the leaves are starting to wilt regardless of what you do, and if you can't see any other problems on the surface, then the problem may be lying underground. There may be some evidence of adult beetle attacks on your bonsai if the leaves have been eaten. You can differentiate a beetle's bite marks from those of caterpillars or snails by the fact that beetle's eat notches into leaves instead of in circular patterns. The indicative U-shape holes are normally created by beetles.

Cure: If your bonsai is looking unhealthy and there is evidence of this, it's best to remove the tree from its pot and inspect the roots. It will be easy to spot any grubs in the root system and they can easily be removed by hand.

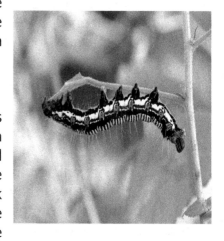

- *Scale*

Description: Scale pests are insects that come in a variety of shapes, sizes, and colors. These insects range from white to yellow to black and even though they move around a lot when they're younger, they tend to find one place that they're comfortable in when they're nearing adulthood and then hunker down and dig into the flesh of the plant they are on.

Once they have burrowed through the protective layers of the plant, they start to drink the sap, but unlike other insects, these stay put and don't move once they have found their spot.

Symptoms: Because they take up permanent residence on one site and have a shiny covering, they resemble scales.

Cure: The best treatment for these types of infections is to physically remove them by hand. Because the insects don't move, they are easy to scrape off with your fingernails and then rinse off. Once you have removed all of the scales it's advisable to apply some bonsai cut cream to the areas to prevent infection.

- *Snails and Slugs*

Description: Everyone has probably seen slugs and snails in the gardens at some point or another and these pests can be very destructive to plant life. They thrive in damp conditions and are most common during the warm, rainy seasons.

Symptoms: Even though they are very slow-moving, they are able to strip an entire bonsai of its leaves in a matter of hours.

Cure: The best treatment against these pests is to go out at night with a flashlight and search for them. Because they are mostly nocturnal, they are very active at night and they like to move around more in cooler temperatures, so they will come out of hiding. If you suspect that there may be a problem in your garden or around your bonsais, then a bit of nocturnal hunting may do the trick to protect your bonsais.

- *Laniger aphid and white cochineal*

Description: They are small insects that develop at the expense of the plant, surrounding themselves with a white waxy substance and feeding on the sap.

Symptoms: White and woolly formations wrap around the petioles of the leaves and the divergence of the branches, weakening the plant.

Cure: use Sanium to spray the synthetic insecticide with the special nebulizer holding the dispenser in a vertical position at 30 - 40 cm - 13- 14 inch, from the plant, treat at the first symptoms of infestation.

Use the spray to wet the plant and apply the product all over the plant.

A single application of the product protects the plant for 8 weeks.

It resists washout and rain, or another spray.

- *Black aphid*

Description: It is an insect that lives in colonies, spreading especially in spring and creating blackish formations attached to sheets and flowers. This slows down the development of the plant in the affected areas.

Symptoms: Dark windings hit the shoots and stretch to the leaves and flowers.

Cure: Use Sanium to spray the synthetic insecticide with the special nebulizer holding the dispenser in a vertical position at 30 - 40 cm 13-14 inch, from the plant, treat at the first symptoms of infestation.

Use the spray to wet the plant and apply the product all over the plant.

A single application of the product protects the plant for 8 weeks.

It resists washout and rain, or another spray.

- *Cochineal*

Description: It is a particular insect and can be of two types. It looks like a shield, dark brown or black with a diameter ranging from 1 to 3 mm and looks like, in a reduced form, conical shells that we find at the seaside, on the rocks, and which are impossible to detach with the fingers. Otherwise, this insect may have the shape of a cotton ball a few millimeters large.

It is an insect that feeds on the sap of plants, injecting a chemical substance inside that causes an abundant secretion of sugars.

This insect positions itself in a point of the trunk, of a branch, of a leaf or external root (i.e. outside the earth), sticks a rostrum in the chosen point and remains there to suck lymph for all its life. Its peculiarity consists in the fact that once it has found the right place, it covers with a waxy substance that makes it unassailable by any anti-insect product. You can find it on the trunk, in the joints of the branches, on the petioles of the leaves or in the leaves themselves, on the veins. It is highly voracious and can cause the death of the plant in a short time. The only way to know if there are mealybugs is to carefully look at many points of the tree, in the period, as for the aphids, between May and September. If on the leaves they are well visible because they are thick black points or white fluffy balls, on the trunk, it is more difficult because the dark type, at times, can be confused with the bark. To find out if what you have seen is a knot in the wood or a mealybug, there is a very simple and effective trick: take a pin and prick the affected point; if it is wood you will not pierce it, while if it is a mealybug the needle will sink into the body of the insect. Pass it to the other side of the shield and detach the insect from the wood. Now you can calmly observe it: that's a mealybug.

Symptoms: In the lower part of the leaves dark-colored folds are created.

Care: the substance you need to buy to cure your bonsai is a white oil-based anticoccidial. White oil is a synthetic mineral oil that dissolves the waxy layer of the mealybug and then, like an insecticide, kills it. Are you coming to the United States? Prepare the solution as indicated on the package and then spray (with a normal spray) all over the tree (not on the ground), without exaggerating the dose. Repeat the operation after a week, after a month and once in winter. At this point, the tree should be free from mealybugs. Clean the infested spots with a cotton swab moistened with alcohol and remove the dead insects that are still on the trunk, branches and leaves. A tip: the bigger the insect, the greater the layer of wax it produces on its body and consequently more difficult to dissolve, so before applying the white oil, take the pin and with patience, remove the insects that are enough large to be skewered. The mealybug is a typical example of an animal attack, difficult to eradicate; fortunately, it is even rarer than an aphid attack.

Alternatively It would sometimes be sufficient to remove the animals from the plant with a simple stick, Alternatively however, the use Sanium to spray the synthetic insecticide with the special nebulizer holding the dispenser in a vertical position at 30 - 40 cm - 13- 14 inch, from the plant, treat at the first symptoms of infestation. Use the spray to wet the plant and apply the product all over the plant. A single application of the product protects the plant for 8 weeks.

It resists washout and rain, or another spray.

- *Earthworms*

Description: Everyone knows the earthworm, a quiet little animal that stays in the damp earth and is good for plants as long as, for the reasons mentioned above, they are not Bonsai.

You may notice earthworms in the soil of the pot especially if the Bonsai is in a garden or nursery. Let's not kill them, these little animals are really useful, not only for fishermen, but also in open spaces such as vegetable gardens, fields or gardens, since they provide very welcome substances to plants.

Treatment: Prepare a solution composed of 4 parts of water and one part of vinegar and water the plant. Eventually, repeat the operation after 3 days. If earthworms are actually there, they will come out of the pot very quickly and maybe even a little altered. Grab them gently and take them to a vegetable garden or a field. The game is done.

- *Phylloxeraradicicol*

Description: It is a female aphid of small size, green or yellow-brown, which lays a large number of eggs and attacks the roots of plants.

Symptoms: The plant tends to turn yellow and deteriorate.

Looking at the roots or the earth, one can notice small gray-white ball formations.

Cure: use Sanium to spray the synthetic insecticide with the special nebulizer holding the dispenser in a vertical position at 30 - 40 cm - 13- 14 inch, from the plant, treat at the first symptoms of infestation. Use the spray to wet the plant and apply the product all over the plant. A single application of the product protects the plant for 8 weeks. It resists washout and rain, or another spray.

- **Whitefly or Aleuroids**

Description: The whitefly is a white insect whose larvae, hidden under the leaves, feed on the sap of the plant, forcing it to emit various sugary productions. It mainly affects plants such as Lantana and Segerezia.

Symptoms: The leaves begin to turn yellow at the bottom and weaken.

Care: the use of products such as JUVINAL 10 EC is recommended

Fill the sprayer tank halfway with water and start the agitator; pour the required dose of product and bring to the desired volume by pouring the remaining amount of water. Keep the agitator running during the transport and use phases.

- *Lice or aphids*

Description: Lice and aphids are insects that live in rather large groups, attaching themselves to the trunk and leaves to suck the sap. Some species are equipped with wings and, moving from plant to plant, they also favor the spread of viruses. **Symptoms:** Insect groups cover leaves and buds that weaken and decay.

Cure: use Sanium to spray the synthetic insecticide with the special nebulizer holding the dispenser in a vertical position at 30 - 40 cm - 13- 14 inch, from the plant, treat at the first symptoms of infestation. Use the spray to wet the plant and apply the product all over the plant. A single application of the product protects the plant for 8 weeks. It resists washout and rain, or another spray.

- ### *Red spider or garden mite*

Description: They are small red, yellow or brown spiders that make their nests on the leaves on the branches. They attack both fruit trees and plants of other species.

Symptoms: The leaves are wrapped in very thin cobwebs on which it is possible to notice animals with a lens. Over time the leaves turn yellow and weaken.

Cure: We recommend using Tetagril on the ground, or spraying the plant with special Lizetan or spray the plant with Neem oil and potassium soft soap. A natural insecticide killer that allows you to eliminate and control soft-bodied insects on plants and also in the soil in a natural and eco-sustainable way.

Plant pests are caused by particularly weak plant conditions that facilitate the spread of diseases.

- ### *Chlorosis*

The most impatient of you, or perhaps those who have less time, will water with the water that has just come out of the tap at home. Certainly, and it is only a matter of time, due to the action of the chlorine present in the water, yellow leaves will appear on the plant, gradually fading to green towards the petiole, as if the leaves were empty of lymph, an unequivocal sign of chlorosis.

The best thing would be to leave the water to rest but if you really don't have time, add iron chelate (or liquid iron) to the watering every 15 days.

Liquid iron chelate, ready to be diluted in water, is readily available.

Keep in mind that the signs that the plant provides us when it is not well are very similar to each other. I have tried to be as clear as possible, indicating all the probable signals that the plant can give you. If you recognize what is described and do not solve the problem with the systems mentioned, then it is very easy that the plant has been attacked by something else.

Description: It is a disease due to a lack of iron or excess calcium in the soil. Factors that prevent easy absorption of mineral substances cause a serious deficiency of chlorophyll inside the plant.

Symptoms: The leaves begin to turn yellow, but leave the ribs green, and wither.

Cure: Before watering, pour Fetrilon or Sequestrene into the right amount.

● *Sooty mold*

Description: They are fungi that affect the bonsai in the trunk, in the leaves and the branches, giving rise to dark incrustations. Mushrooms often feed on sugary substances caused by the passage of aphids and above all are favored by high humidity and poor ventilation.

Symptoms: Dark-colored spots or sooty areas are created in the affected areas.

Cure: We recommend the use of Cupravit or Baymat, or in any case of any product with copper oxychloride.

● Radical rot

Description: We will realize that we have given too much water to the plant from the following signs: the earth is always soggy, the leaves begin to yellow, then turn brown and fall.

Symptoms: The best treatment for this problem is prevention. It is best to not overwater your bonsai and also keep the ground in the pot clear of any fallen foliage. Sometimes, infected leaves can drop onto the soil and infect it with a fungus, so it's best to remove them when you notice some leaves have died and fallen off. It is also necessary to ensure that your tree is an area that is well-ventilated and has decent exposure to sunlight. Try to stop watering for a few days. If the roots have not been damaged, that is, they have not rotted, the tree will absorb excess water and the earth will dry out.

At this point, resume watering, but in a reduced way. If, however, you see that the earth does not dry out and the plant continues to lose its leaves, it means that the root system is damaged: the plant must be repotted immediately, removing soaked earth and rotten roots, and planted in fresh and dry earth.

Then the watering will be suspended for about 5/6 days, resuming them gradually starting from small doses. If the plant is tough enough it should recover and new buds should emerge from the leafless branches. But be aware that the recovery of the plant, after such a shock, is often a matter of luck.

Warning: repotting is a rather meticulous operation due to the many things to pay attention to such as the type of soil to use, the tying of the plant in the pot, etc.

If you suspect that your bonsai may have root rot, it is best to remove your bonsai from its pot and prune away all of the infected roots. This may or not work because of the severity of the fungal spread, but it is worth the try. Once all of the infected roots have been pruned, the tree needs to be planted in fast-draining soil.

The roots rot mainly for two reasons: Excessive fertilization, which causes damage and necrosis, and an excessively abundant watering, which causes water to stagnate in the soil.

Root rot is a problem that all bonsais face because they spend their lives in pots. This problem is caused by a fungus because of poor drainage in the pot. Plants and trees that are planted in the ground don't usually face this problem but it is a risk for any potted tree or plant.

As soon as the water starts to back up and the roots sit in unnecessary fluid, they become much softer and at risk for fungal infections. If roots turn brown and take on a mushy-like consistency, the tree won't be able to draw up water and nutrients any longer and the tree will inevitably die.

It is important to note that not all fungi in roots are bad things and root rot shouldn't be confused with the white fungus that grows in the roots of pine trees because that fungus is absolutely essential to the pine trees' survival.

The plant weakens and begins to perish, due to the Tadice's inability to forfeit nourishment, the leaves take on a dark color.

Cure:

Severe root rot can be treated with Lime Sulfur, a broad-acting fungicide, and it may be able to kill the fungus. If there are roots still strong enough to heal, there still may be a chance of survival. But it's definitely best not to let it get to this point and rather prevent it from occurring altogether.

It is good to cut the sick and already dead roots and leave the healthy ones in a solution of Benomyl or Orthocid, after having cleaned them well from the ground.

Kiplantate the bonsai in a pot with new soil, keeping the soil watered and moist fertilizing should be practiced only after 2 months.

It can happen, especially in the early days, to make a mistake in dosing the watering of the plant, causing it some problems.

- *Withering*

If, on the other hand, there is little watering, the plant will show it very quickly, (the layer below the surface of the earth dries after a few hours) initially bending down the leaves which will then wither.

If we are really deaf to the calls of the tree, cracks will also form in the earth which will then detach from the inner edges of the vase. The first reaction would be to put a lot of water in the earth, "So it drinks!" Nothing worse than that. If you get to this point, the roots of the plant wouldn't be capable of absorbing water and generous watering would do no good. First, equip yourself with a nebulizer and vaporize the water on all the leaves, wetting them well. Then take a transparent cellophane bag and keeping the opening downwards, insert the Bonsai's foliage and with a piece of string close the bag, loosely, tying it in the lower part of the trunk.

Now, with the nebulizer, spray a few times on the earth letting it absorb the water: the very fine droplets of the vaporizer are able to be absorbed even by very dry earth, which wouldn't be possible by normal watering. Make cuts more or less one centimeter long in the bag, with scissors, so that the plant can also breathe; the leaves that you see withered, are actually still alive and able to carry out the chlorophyll synthesis even if in a reduced way. Every day, for a week, spray the earth and the foliage, spraying the latter from one of the holes in the bag. After a week, water the earth normally and when you see the leaves recover, or you notice new buds sprouting from the branches, remove the bag and let air in; your plant is safe.

- *Powdery mildew or Spaerotheca*

Description: They are also fungi that affect the plant in particular conditions of temperature and ventilation. Their propagation is facilitated by the particular heat and humidity, so it is good to be particularly careful in the summer.

Symptoms: Powdery mildew creates a whitish powder-like substance on the front of the leaves and in the other affected points, gradually weakening the plant.

Cure: To eliminate powdery mildew in a short time, you can use any fungicide or even a KB solution of micronized sulfur to be administered every 15 days.

● *False powdery mildew*

Description: It is a mushroom similar to the previous one, even if it manifests itself differently way. It is favored by inadequate conditions of temperature and humidity.

Symptoms: It determines a gray moldy substance in the lower part of the leaves, while it turns yellow the upper one, staining some points of gray.

Cure: Use Bayleton or CupravitBlu, spraying it in the relevant points, transporting the bonsai to a well-ventilated place

● *Virosis*

Description: These are all the diseases caused by the spread of viruses which, however, are still not easily identifiable today and which often occur in a deleterious way for plants.

The virus spreads easily or through insects, or due to infected tools, or in any circumstance in which some wounds of the tree can be affected, such as in the case of grafts, pruning, etc.

Symptoms: The symptoms are various and are not always recognizable in a short time. In the most common cases, these are streaks of various colors that are highlighted on the leaves; regardless of the symptoms the fate of the plant is however probably sealed.

Cure: Unfortunately, there are few remedies after a plant has been affected.

You can only try to make sure that the infection does not expand, moving the plant away. Above all, however, it is recommended to prevent virosis by fighting animal parasites and keeping tools clean.

PROBLEMS DUE TO THE ENVIRONMENT

Due to the lack of information, one of the most frequent reasons for the death of a Bonsai is the wrong location.

The environmental rules valid for plants in nature must be respected. In this chapter, I will refer much more often to the winter location, which is the most critical, rather than to the summer one, where the main thing (but not less important) is to provide light to the Bonsai.

Let's clarify, first of all, one thing: plants that live well indoors are rare even if it is a common desire to have a splendid tree in our home, perhaps in little light or near a heater. Let us briefly recall some rules of botany. Plants feel winter, that is that period of vegetative stasis, rest. Let's make a strange comparison: let's admit that the tree lives a day that lasts one of our years. The plant wakes up in the morning (spring) rested and with the energy to start a new day, then in the afternoon it is full of its energy (summer) and works until it feels tired in the evening (autumn) and then it prepares to rest during the night (winter) and gets ready to start a new day.

If we spend a night awake, at work, we will find ourselves

completely dazed the next morning and, surely, we will not perform as well as after a night of sleep. What keeps a plant awake all night (or winter) is the heat in the apartment. The following spring we will have a tree that is certainly in bad condition.

It is therefore extremely important to know where to place the plant during the various periods of the year in order to always have the best results from the tree (therefore an always beautiful Bonsai) without forcing it and without tiring it.

Bonsai, therefore, must always be placed in an environment suitable for its needs. Each species requires a certain amount of light, humidity, temperature, which must be guaranteed overtime for the good health of the plant. Let's see together how to give our bonsai the optimal environment.

There are multiple things that you may need to consider when dealing with growing your bonsai but the three most important factors that you need to keep in mind (regardless of where you are in the world) are light, humidity, and temperature.

If you have locally sourced your seeds it is advisable to keep your bonsai outdoors because it's in an environment that it will thrive in, but if you are growing a non-indigenous bonsai, then it may be necessary to keep your bonsai indoors to better control the factors it is exposed to.

Temperature

Most bonsais prefer slightly warmer climates during their growing periods and they will require slightly warmer temperatures in the spring and summer months. It is perfectly healthy if you wish for your bonsai to go dormant in the colder months but during the spring and summer, it is best to keep your bonsai at temperatures between 68 and 86 degrees F. (20 to 30 degrees Celsius).

Keeping your bonsai at this temperature will allow for it to stay healthy while it's indoors and since it's indoors there will be a lower chance of pests and other infections attacking your bonsai, provided the ventilation, watering, and fertilizing are occurring well.

It is good to always keep in mind the temperature of the original place of the plant and try to recreate it also in our apartment.

Plants are classified into two groups, depending on their origin and needs: Tropical plants and subtropical plants.

Tropical plants need during the day temperature between 18 and 24 degrees Celsius - 64.4-75,2 F.; at night it is better not to drop below 15-16 degrees Celsius – 60 F..

The subtropical plants, on the other hand, do not bear a too hot climate, and I prefer minimum temperatures in winter between 5 and 12 degrees Celsius - 41-53,6 F..

Not respecting these needs of the plant means causing them serious damage.

In general, the cold causes a slowdown in growth, chlorosis, cracking of the branches or the trunk, the death of the leaves, even the death of all the bonsai.

It also happens if the temperature is too hot with the risk the plant ends up drying out.

We, therefore, recommend keeping bonsai in a suitable place: Tropical plants are usually placed on heating sources or as close as possible, to exploit their heat throughout the day.

At night it is good to take them to a slightly cooler place, to cause a natural temperature, drop of 5-6 degrees Celsius – 41-42.8 F..

Subtropical plants are more suitable for winter gardens, cool rooms, or in the corridor.

Also, in this case, it is recommended to provide a slight drop in temperature during the night by bringing the plant near the window or in a cooler place.

It is good, however, that the temperature changes are not excessive.

If you intend to place the plants in the open air for the summer, it will be better not to expose them directly to sunlight, they will necessarily be collected at home when the night temperature starts to drop below I degrees.

It may happen that a Bonsai is placed, in summer, in a too sunny place and that it gets sunstroke. We will notice this (especially if it is a maple, even more so if it is a Japanese maple) because the leaves will first become dry to the touch and then wither until the plant looks dead. Here's how we should behave: take a pair of sharp scissors and cut all the dry leaves in half petiole (for the uninitiated the petiole is the thread that connects the leaf to the branch).

Make supplemental fertilization with a dose of nitrogen (if you haven't already done it), and water the plant. In the following days, water in a reduced way, nebulize the branches and any remaining leaves and keep the Bonsai in a place sheltered from the strong sun, but in the light. When you notice that the buds on the branches begin to open, remove the bag and start watering the Bonsai again but do not move it from where it is until it has completely opened the new leaves. For this period, it is important to leave the plant in a place sheltered from the strong sun as the young leaves are extremely sensitive and vulnerable to too intense heat.

Light

Everyone knows that plants need light to live, but many believe that it is enough just to guarantee the tree its functions.

Plants in general, apart from a few exceptions which in any case do not concern Bonsai, need a lot of light. For example, a closed balcony that is made of concrete and without iron bars, covered by a canopy-type curtain, does not guarantee the light necessary for the survival of any essence. After some time you will see the leaves of the Bonsai turn yellow and then fall inexorably causing the plant to die. I recommend balconies not protected by awnings that darken, or window sills (which do not look south, in summer the sun is too strong); lucky those who have a garden available.

Plants speak to us: if the leaves tend to all point in the same direction, going in the opposite direction to the natural growth and the course of the branch, it means that the plant wants more light.   .

Plants, as we know, have a great need for light to be able to start the process of photosynthesis, but in this case, too it is good not to exceed.

The excess of light in especially if the plant is not used to it can cause the discoloration of the leaves and a consequent weakening of the plant. We, therefore, recommend keeping the bonsai in a bright place, without it being directly exposed to the sun's rays.

If you are planning on keeping your bonsai inside because you know you will spend more time with it like that, you will need to find a way to get it to receive enough UV light.

In the home it is often necessary to use artificial light to integrate the one coming from outside; in this case, it is better to avoid normal incandescent bulbs because they emit light too different from the solar one.

If the plant has little light, you will notice that the leaves take on an unnatural color. It will no longer be a beautiful deep green, but a faded green, with yellow and brown flecks.

This happens for a consistent failure of the chlorophyll synthesis

One of the greatest difficulties of keeping a tropical bonsai indoors is ensuring that it is exposed to enough light with a high enough intensity.

We   recommend quartz and iodine lamps and fluorescent tubes for aquariums.

Trees are resilient and they won't die immediately if their ideal conditions aren't met, but their health will deteriorate over time. Therefore, it is much better to ensure that your bonsai has enough light from the very beginning.

Placing your bonsai in front of a window that receives a lot of sunlight will greatly benefit your bonsai in the long run, so choosing the right window is paramount to your bonsai's overall success. Some windows may seem light enough but they may not receive the correct amount of UV ray concentration needed for a healthy bonsai. Windows situated at the east or west of the house will be ideal because they will receive the morning or afternoon sun.

That being said, this is for bonsais from tropical climates, and some trees can function with indirect light, so adequate research is always necessary.

Twilight

If it is true that light is an indispensable element for the growth of your tree, it is equally true that many times serious damage is caused precisely by a heat blow to the leaves caused by too strong sun.

The ideal solution during summer would be to keep the plants in an open place, under a pergola made with bamboo canes. It would also be an excellent choice to put your Bonsai under a tree, which guarantees shade during the warmer hours of the day.

Logically not everyone has a garden with trees or a place where to mount a pergola, so if possible keep the plants on balconies, in a point where there is no direct light during hot hours.

The same thing also applies to the window sills, they are excellent if arranged in all directions except to the south since, at this point, in summer, the sun beats strongest until around 2 pm.

An optimal place would be one where the plant has direct light only in the morning until 11 am or in the afternoon starting from 3 pm.

Do not be frightened by timetables, cardinal points and light issues: stop and think, finding a suitable place for your plant.

Two tips: when you put a Bonsai on the balcony, place it on a small wooden plank to protect the roots from the heat coming from the concrete, which is very harmful, and if you use a window sill, I recommend you to find a way to fix the pot well.

Humidity

Some trees thrive in humidity, while others prefer drier climates. But most bonsais function fairly well with increased humidity levels because they can draw from the moisture in the air. The only challenge with this is that some bonsais may require humidity levels that are higher than those in your house, especially if you have air-conditioners or heaters running.

You may think that you will need to buy a humidifier for your bonsai, but a simple tray of water next to the tree can create some vapor as it stands in the sunlight or a regular misting with a spray bottle is also sufficient. As long as your bonsai receives water vapor from the air, it will grow very well.

As it is easy to guess, two factors can come into play by damaging the plant, if not kept under constant control: The humidity of the air and the watering.

Most bonsai need a humidity of between 40 and 50%.

If the bonsai is placed in a too dry place, the plant evaporates more water than it manages to forfeit from the roots, causing a decrease in growth and risking the leaves, branches and trunk to dry out.

On the contrary, on the other hand, if the humidity is excessive, there is a danger of a general weakening of the plant, of the spread of parasitic diseases such as fungi, up to the possibility that the whole plant will rot. As we said, watering also plays an important role and should be practiced in moderation.

Excess water with bad drainage in the soil facilitates root rot, fungi and pests. It also decreases the speed of development of the plant, causing it asphyxiation and heaviness.

It is therefore better to water often, but in moderate quantities, rather than rarely in large quantities. It is also good to make sure that the water does not stagnate in the pot, but has an easy outlet thanks to the drainage holes.

Indoor and outdoor bonsai

As said before, there are very few plants that can stay indoors in winter and, in any case, must be kept in certain conditions in order to survive.

Let's say in general that all those plants originating from a hot and humid climate such as tropical can be kept indoors.

Plants suitable for domestic location are Ficus benjamina, Ficus retusa and all cultivars (cultivars are the subspecies of every single variety of plant) belonging to this family except the Ficus which is the common fruit fig which, accustomed to our climates, loves low temperatures during winter.

We can also choose a Schefflera arborescens, a plant well known for its home ornamental use and truly splendid if grown as Bonsai.

Other suitable plants are Carmona microphylla or tea plant, Serissa foetida (pronounced "fetida", from Latin foetïdus, smelly, and by plucking a leaf and smelling it you will understand the reason for this name) and sagerezia (Sageretia theezan), one of the essences inherited from the Chinese.

All the other plants are outdoor plants, be they broad-leaved or coniferous.

The elm, the lime tree, the hornbeam, the poplar, the zelkova, the maple, the oak, the privet, the boxwood, the forsythia, the wisteria, the cotoneaster, the pyracanta, the hawthorn, the holly, the olive tree, apple tree, pear tree, apricot tree, peach tree are just some of the numerous broad-leaved trees that must overwinter in the cold.

As far as conifers are concerned, I name pines, firs, cedars, larch, junipers, yew, etc. But when is it winter? And when is it cold for the plant?

When the temperature drops below 5 degrees (attention: even for just a few hours) then the plant is cold and feels the "winter", although a tree can resist very well to a temperature of 2° C-35, 6 ° F.

But the real danger is not for the plant itself, or at least for what we see of the plant. The real risk is the roots: if the earth in the pot, when the temperature reaches 0° C., -32° F., freezes, the plant would be certainly doomed.

DISEASES DUE TO EXCESS OR LACK OF NUTRIENTS

Plants can also get sick when the soil does not adequately contain all the elements necessary for nourishment. The bonsai highlights particular symptoms that can become real diseases if you don't try to live the problem immediately with adequate fertilizer. Often, then, the lack of water causes serious damage to leaves and flowers, such as the drying out of the log edges, deformation and fall of the shoots, etc. On the contrary, too much water prevents the soil from breathing, causing root rot.

Now we will examine the nutrients that can cause damage to the plant if they are not present in the necessary quantity.

- *Nitrogen*

If the soil contains an excessive amount of nitrogen, the tree tends to accelerate its development speed, but this causes a weakening of the plant and a lower ability to defend against disease and cold. If instead the percentage of nitrogen is lower, the development slows down and the vegetative cycle is shortened, to the detriment of leaves and shoots.

- *Boron*

The lack of boron damages the leaves which weaken, drying out easily.

The plant deteriorates and does not grow.

- *Iron*

Iron in small quantities causes the leaves to turn yellow and weaken the plant.

- ### Phosphorus

The lack of phosphorus in the soil causes the plant to stop developing, giving the leaves a bronze color and making them leathery.

- ### Magnesium

The lack of magnesium in the soil gives the leaves red and chlorosis coloring.

- ### Potassium

When the plant lacks the right amount of potassium, serious damage to the leaves occurs. They begin to curl on the edges and turn dark and rot; the whole plant suffers, weakening its defenses.

- ### Zinc

Be careful to give the right dose of fertilizer. When you fertilize the plant with nitrogen, you can see the results almost immediately, in a few days, especially on certain essences, such as elm, which are the jets of new leaves, even 3 or 4 cm long.

Taken by the euphoria of seeing the plant so sprightly, it is tempting to fertilize more increasing the doses. This must not be done: a little fertilizer is of little use, while too much can burn the leaves. If you happen to unload an excessive dose of fertilizer (and you will notice it because the edges of the leaves turn brown), suspend the administration for a couple of months and reduce the watering doses for about 10 days.

The plant should recover quickly and replace any lost leaf. Too large a dose of fertilizer (double or triple) can also kill the plant, but, if you have not exaggerated, you will get at most a little scorched leaves until the following year.

The plant slows down its development, with the consequence that the leaves remain small and thin and easily affected by chlorosis.

INJURIES AND WOUNDS

Let's talk now about how-to bring relief to the plant in case of injuries caused by diseases or by bad use of tools.

It is first of all important to try to prevent the possibility of injury by keeping the bonsai in a sheltered place, where there is no risk of damage. Also, it is always good to keep the tools in good condition and, during pruning, make a clean and flat cut, to limit the extent of the wound to a minimum.

Plants have a great natural healing ability, however, always good to help them by applying waxes and pastes that contain healing hormones such as Lac balsam or other products readily available on the market.

In case there are dead or infected parts, it is good to remove them immediately, in order to facilitate the recovery of the plant.

Furthermore, during the vegetative period and especially when it is very hot, the plant must be followed in a particular way because it is more active and more willing to infections.

CHAPTER 6

Containers And Tools

The choice of the container can compromise or enhance the overall harmony of bonsai creation. An ideal container can bring out a plant without particular value, hiding its defects and highlighting its most peculiar characteristics.

Usually, they are made in porcelain or terracotta and it is not uncommon to find vitrified models on the outside.

However, the containers on the market offer such a variety, of colors and sizes, that the choice is not always easy. However, some rules can help us.

The suitable dimensions depend on those of the bonsai: The pot must be at least two-thirds of the height of the trunk and the height should not be less than the thickness of the trunk.

As for the color, we usually tend to create particular contrasts between the container and the tree, as required by the principle of asymmetric balancing. So, for trees with dark foliage, vases with light colors will be used mostly and vice versa.

This rule is however subject to the taste of the bonsai artist, who may deem preferable, which among other things, in some cases is necessary for a good overall object. Each style prefers a certain shape of the container:

- **Moyogi:** Oval, shallow, round, shallow and rectangular containers can be used.

- **Chokkan:** Shallow, oval and rectangular square pots are to be used.

- **Shakan:** Shallow, round, shallow and rectangular shapes are recommended.

- **Kengai:** Containers must be very deep rounds to allow the tree to develop properly alongside the pot.

- **Sokan:** The containers can be oval and round low

- **Sankan:** The recommended containers are the low shapeless ones.

- **Vahudachi:** Low round, rectangular and low shapeless vases are used.

- **Ikada:** Oval and low-form ones are suitable.

- **Netsuranari:** Shapeless low vessels are recommended.

- **Vose-ue:** The containers must be oval, rectangular or low-form.

- **Hokidachi:** Oval, shallow square, low round and shallow, rectangular and low shapeless containers are to be used.

- **Fukinagashi:** The recommended shapes are oval, shallow square, low round and shallow and rectangular.

- **Bunjingi**: Low and shallow round pots are recommended.

- **Ishitsuki**: The oval, low round and rectangular vases fit.

- **Saikei and Bonkei:** It is preferable to use low oval and rectangular vases, even if all those containers that enhance the general composition are suitable.

- **Han-Kengai:** Use deep or very deep square or very deep round vases.

The use of containers with feet is preferable, because keeping the vase raised concerning the support surface, it allows better air circulation and more easy expulsion of water.

Often the bonsai are placed on special wooden display tables or mobile shelves. The latter, which is useful for moving the plant when necessary, can also be easily built on their own.

ARRANGEMENT OF BONSAI IN THE CONTAINER

FORMA

ALTEZZA

BORDO   PIEDINI

After having seen the variety of containers, let's now see together some general advice on which arrangement is best to give the bonsai in their container.

To facilitate the exposure, it is good to make a first distinction between the front and the back of the bonsai. The front is visible to the observer.

It will be necessary, therefore, to choose as the front of the bonsai that part that does not have branches directed towards the observer, to give an orderly and accurate impression to the composition.

Usually, then the roots that emerge from the ground are also placed towards the front, to give an idea of greater stability to the whole plant.

It is also essential to distinguish between straight trunk trees, leaning trunk trees and groups of trees.

Each of these cases will follow different rules:

- *Straight trunk trees:* if your style includes trees with a straight trunk, you will need to arrange the trunk so that it is moved a little back from the center of the pot and slightly inclined towards you. This will result in a lively look, accentuating the shape of the canopy relative to the trunk

- *Tree with leaning trunk:* The inclination of the tree must always be oriented right to left or the other way around. In case the tree leans to the right, you will have to move the base of the trunk to the left of the container. Otherwise, instead, you have to move the trunk to the right of the container. Also, for this group of trees, it is advisable to bring a slight inclination towards the front

- *Groups of trees:* If you have chosen trees that have double or multiple trunks coming from the same root, these will always be arranged in the center of the container. If instead the trees are autonomous from each other and you want to make a composition, they can be arranged in a more varied way.

In this regard, however, more information can be found in the chapter dedicated to group styles.

BONSAI TOOLS

Let's now describe the main tools to be used in the maintenance and transformation of bonsai. For those who are preparing to start growing a bonsai, the following tools are needed:

1.   A plastic or metal watering can equip with replaceable onions with a flat and inclined face. The first provides a strong enough jet, useful for watering leaves and foliage. The second is to be used to water the soil as it makes the water flow more gently.

2.   A pair of elongated bonsai pruning shears. The length of these elongated allows you to work inside the foliage very easily.

3.   A pair of wide scissors, useful for truncating large roots. A bonsai hacksaw can also be used for this purpose.

4.   A pair of concave shears, useful for cutting branches to obtain a section as regular as possible, facilitating wound healing.

5.   Mesh in thin mesh to be placed over the drainage holes, to prevent lumps of earth from coming out.

6.   Aluminum wire to wrap branches and trunk, in case you want to change its shape.

7.   A small wire cutter to cut the wire without injuring the bark.

8.   A stick or a paperclip to clean the roots from the ground and separate them during repotting.

9.   A rake to level the ground.

10.   A broom to clean.

It is essential to remember to carefully clean each tool after use to avoid the spread of germs or diseases. For this purpose, it is possible to find types of disinfectants for tools on the market.

CHAPTER 7

Tips and Information

Keeping a bonsai may be something that excites and frightens you at the same time and since there are so many things you need to remember, it may feel overwhelming. But it is important for you as an enthusiast to work with your bonsai in the ways that you feel fit, and also keep in mind that you don't always have to keep an eye on it. Some enthusiasts are worried about leaving their bonsai for a few days because they're worried something may go wrong during that period, but there is little risk.

If you are going away for a few days, then it's fine to give your bonsai slightly more water than you normally would. A single watering that's slightly more than normal isn't going to hurt the tree, and just ensure that you have fertilized it too before leaving (if you are going away in the summer months). But, if you are leaving for slightly longer periods of time, then it's best to give the bonsai to someone you trust with a set of instructions on how to water and feed it.

When the holiday season arrives, you will face the problem of how to behave with bonsai, where to leave it, whom to leave it, etc. Always comes up.

The ideal would be to have someone to whom to entrust him who is able to replace our care for the necessary period, however, this is not always possible. In the event that the absence is short-lived, lasting up to a week, then the bonsai can be left alone, even if it is necessary to prepare a suitable place to keep it moist all the time. It will be sufficient to bury the pot inside a larger container that has a layer of wet peat. Otherwise, you can create a small greenhouse with a transparent plastic bag inside which to insert the pot. The bag will be closed over the bonsai after it has been watered abundantly. It is also necessary to drill holes in the plastic to circulate the air while maintaining the necessary humidity inside.

For longer periods, a connection can be made between a container full of water, placed higher up, and the bonsai pot using a tube that slowly brings water to a wedge planted in the soil.

To obtain the same result in an easier way, a simple woolen thread can be used instead of the tube and the wedge impregnating the water with the thread, it will slowly let it drop on the ground.

However, even in this case, a person's assistance would be needed to check that everything is going well and to solve any problems that could arise.

There may be times that your bonsai gets hurt because of a mistake you made or because something happened to it. Remember that accidents happen but you will be able to solve many of these problems with the correct tools. Before starting to grow your bonsai, it's advisable to get a bonsai kit so you can have the clippers, wire, cut-cream, and bonsai scissors. If you have these items, taking care of your bonsai won't be difficult.

If your bonsai gets a damaged trunk, treat it as you would a wound on yourself. Place the cut-cream on the wound and wrap it with bonsai tape and plastic wrap to protect it from infection. This method can be used from anything from grafts to a trunk that's been split.

The final tip is to trust yourself and always do your research on the bonsais that you are keeping. You won't know everything about bonsais in the beginning, but you are able to know a lot about the bonsais you are currently keeping or interested in growing in the future.

1) Watering by subtracting the bonsai pot in a moist soil;   2) Watering through a wire of wool connected to a basin of water;

3)Greenhouse made with plastic bag

1)

2)

3)

Conclusion

There are numerous topics concerning the wonderful world of Bonsai that we have not mentioned.

There are many things to learn before feeling calm.

Do not worry when you realize you are afraid of cutting a plant, it is a feeling that everyone has experienced, myself included, and that will pass over time with the awareness that nothing or anyone is hurt.

Do not be discouraged by failures, but be modest in front of a victory, it is the best way to face the problems that will come.

If you find, over time, that you do not know enough, go further, read, study, attend technical courses, read up and see that difficulties are nothing compared to the satisfaction you feel. Love your plants, take care of them, enjoy the summer sun with them and watch them sleep in the cold of winter, they will know how to thank you.

Their flowers, their fruits, their awakening, are much more than what you can now imagine.

The art of keeping bonsais must be one of the most rewarding practices in the world today and even though it can take years of your life, it isn't something that you will ever regret doing. Growing bonsais is so much more than just growing a beautiful tree in a pot and looking after it on a daily basis; it is more of a choice that teaches you everything that you need to know about yourself.

It may be difficult to consider that growing a bonsai can take years and once you have shaped, nurtured, and helped grow it into something that you are truly proud of, it may have taken decades of your life. But when you look at the marvelous creations in front of you and your designing capabilities, you will know it was all worth it.

There will be times that you feel that you don't have the patience to perform this type of task but you will surprise yourself as you find yourself becoming more and more at peace with your newfound understanding.

There is a lot of detail in this book and even though you may feel overwhelmed at first, this book is merely just the beginning but it will help guide you along your way. Once you understand the basics of keeping bonsais at a beginner level, there will be nothing stopping you from exploring more difficult and advanced concepts.

Start with single styles and then move into group styles because you need to understand how to safely work with the roots of one tree before you move into dealing with multiple, and treat every individual bonsai that you have with all of the love and patience that you are building within yourself.

All of this will take practice and you are going to make mistakes, but that is the entire process of learning. Once you realize what you are capable of doing, you will want to do more and achieve more with growing these pieces of art.

This is a long journey that you are going to go on and even though it is one of growing trees in pots, it is more about self-discovery and it definitely is one that you are going to love to go on.

I hope, with this book, I have given a small but valid help to those who did not know how to take care of a Bonsai and an important boost to those who one day will become a master of this art. Good job to all.

FAQ

What does 'BONSAI' mean?
The word BONSAI literally means «tree grown in a pot». This word is spelled the same in both Chinese and Japanese.

Can Bonsai be made with all types of trees?
With most, but not all. For example, walnut is a plant that is not suitable to be transformed into Bonsai.

Can Bonsai be kept at home?
There are some essences that adapt to living in the domestic climate, but even these prefer to live outside, in spring and summer. Basically, there are no indoor Bonsai, even if with certain expedients it would be possible to make them live all year round at home; but they are so cumbersome as to be impractical and make the plant suffer.

What type of plant should you choose?
I always recommend the typical essences of the region where you live. Basically, the important thing is to choose a healthy plant.

Does the plant stay small even without doing anything to it?
Absolutely no. Bonsais are very normal trees, made small by common gardening operations. Therefore, if they are not taken care of, they tend to grow.

When I have some guests, can I put the Bonsai on a

piece of furniture, and show it to them?

Yes, but only for a few hours. As soon as possible bring the Bonsai back to the place where it was.

Why is it not necessary to fertilize or trim in August?

Because due to the heat the plants, in August, go into a dormancy similar to the winter one. It is better not to do any operation in this period because it can be harmful to the Bonsai.

Is it better to grow a young plant or an old one?

Both cases have pros and cons. If you choose a young plant, you will have a Bonsai more resistant to any maintenance errors or diseases but, precisely because it is young and very vigorous, you will have to control it so as not to lose its shape. These problems are reversed in a long-standing plant. Furthermore, a young plant is usually even less beautiful than an old one.

How much watering is necessary?

Each plant needs a particular amount of water.

Is snow bad for the plant?

No, but only if the pot is adequately protected from frost.

I have a bag of Bonsai seeds, can I use them?

part from the fact that there are no Bonsai seeds but there are tree seeds that once born and educated, can become Bonsai, if you have patience for at least ten years, yes.

Can I use the fertilizer I use for other indoor plants on Bonsai?

In theory, yes, but it depends on the quantity, in percentage, of the elements contained in the fertilizer.

My apple tree is full of fruit, do I have to leave them all?

It is better to leave a maximum of ten, otherwise, the plant will try too hard and next year it may not bear fruit.

Why does my plant make yellow leaves which then fall off?

Most likely this is caused by an excess of water.

The plant has brown leaf edges, what is it?

Almost certainly an excess of fertilization.

What does it mean if there are ants on the tree?

If the ants are very small, surely the plant is being attacked by aphids.

I put the Bonsai on the ground in the garden for a few days and some roots came out of the holes in the pot, do I have to cut them?

Yes, it is better to remove them, because they could rot. Use a very sharp pair of scissors.

The soil of my Bonsai has become hard, there are cracks and the water is no longer absorbed, what should I do?

The plant must be repotted.

In the middle of the moss of my Bonsai some green growths have grown in the shape of a flower, what are they?

They are lichens, it is a sign that the earth is healthy and the plant is fine, but when lichens grow it also means that there is a lot of moisture in the soil, so be very careful.

Small mushrooms have grown under my oak, do I have to remove them?

No, for heaven's sake; don't eat them but enjoy the show: you have a piece of wood at home.

My oak, in autumn and winter, has all dry leaves, do I have to remove them?

No, oaks and beeches don't drop the leaves, they just dry out. They will fall in spring at the birth of the new ones.

Aphid: small lymph sucking insect.

Expanded clay: balls of mineral material with a diameter ranging 3 and 10 mm, which serve as a layer in the pots and as a support for indoor plants since it moistures them too.

Bonsai: tree grown in a pot, artistically.

Candle: typical gem, characteristic of pines.

Topping: removal of young vegetation aimed at limiting the crown.

Iron chelate: chemical amendment which, dissolved in water, is used for the treatment of chlorosis.

Crown: it is the green (or red) part of the tree, the one formed by the leaves.

Onion: plastic or brass accessory with small holes that, attached to the tip of the watering can, lets the water pour out.

Chlorosis: yellowing of the leaves caused by excess chlorine in the watering.

Mealybug: roundish insect, in the shape of a shield or cotton swab, which positions itself in the folds of the tree and sucks lymph.

Fertilizer: organic soil improver that serves as nourishment for the plant.

Conifers: a family of plants. They can be recognized by the particular shape of the leaves, most of the time needle-like, not flat as in broad-leaved trees.

Cultivar: subspecies of a variety of trees (Siberian elm, leafy elm, English elm, etc.).

Drainage: a layer of expanded clay that is placed in the pot to facilitate the flow of excess water out through the holes in the pot.

Brick effect: excessive hardening of the soil caused by the limestone trope contained in it or by the bad mixture of the soils that form it.

Essence: plant species (oak, linden, apple, pine, etc.).

Aluminum wire: metal wire available in various sizes

(diameters) which is used to shape the Bonsai.

Freezing: lowering of the temperature below 0° which lasts for a few hours or days.

Bud: part of the tree from which branches, leaves or flowers are formed.

Apical bud: bud placed on the tip of a branch.

Watering: operation by which the plant is given the water it needs to live.

Internode: the wood, in a branch, between two leaves.

Jin: dead branch, without bark, left on the tree for beauty.

Broad-leaved trees: a family of trees with more or less large flat leaves.

Slow-release: it is said of solid fertilizer that once placed in the soil releases its nutritional principles, not immediately, but over time.

Lymph: a nutritional liquid that circulates inside plants.

Twilight: an area where, in July and August, there is light but the direct sun does not shine.

Pergola: cover, made of bamboo canes or net, designed to create penumbra.

Petiole: an arboreal stem that attaches the leaf to the branch.

Acid rain: rains with a very low pH, therefore acidic and corrosive, caused by excess pollution in the atmosphere.

Pruning: operation aimed at removing a branch or part of a trunk.

Evergreen: it is said of broad-leaved or coniferous trees that do not lose their leaves in winter.

Cold greenhouse: a protected place where there is light and where, in winter, the temperature never drops below 2°.

Chlorophyll synthesis: the process of assimilation of light and carbon dioxide by the plant, with the production of carbon hydrates.

Stripping: it is said of broad-leaved or coniferous trees that lose their leaves in winter.

Style: shape given to Bonsai following the rules of Japanese masters.

Location: a place to keep the plant.

Dear Reader

I am an emerging writer and, with the sales made by the book, I can continue my studies to publish other books on the subject.

I would appreciate an honest review from you.

Also, please if you notice any mistakes or missing information, feel free to contact me at this e-mail address: daring.limited@gmail.com

Thank you for your support

CPSIA information can be obtained
at www.ICGtesting.com
Printed in the USA
LVHW081534040622
720519LV00015B/643